Differing Visions

Administering Indian Residential Schooling in Prince Albert

1867–1995

Noel Dyck

with a Foreword by
Grand Chief Alphonse Bird

Fernwood Publishing • Halifax
The Prince Albert Grand Council • Prince Albert

Editing: Donna Davis
Cover design: Zoë Dyck
Index: Donna Robertson
Design and production: Beverley Rach
Printed and bound in Canada by: Hignell Printing Limited

A publication of:
Fernwood Publishing
Box 9409, Station A
Halifax, Nova Scotia
B3K 5S3

and

The Prince Albert Grand Council
Prince Albert, Saskatchewan

Fernwood Publishing Company Limited gratefully acknowledges the financial support
of the Ministry of Canadian Heritage and the Nova Scotia Department of Education
and Culture.

Canadian Cataloguing in Publication Data

Main entry under title:

Differing visions

      Includes bibliographical references
      ISBN 1-895686-85-7

1. Indians of North America -- Saskatchewan -- Prince Albert
Region -- Residential schools. * 2. Indians of North America --
Education -- Saskatchewan -- Prince Albert Region -- History.
I. Title.
E96.65.S3D93 1997   371.829'97071242   C97-950084-2

Contents

Acknowledgments / 4

List of Abbreviations / 5

Map / 6

Foreword, by Grand Chief Alphonse Bird / 7

1. Introduction: The Significance of Indian Residential Schooling / 9

2. The Evangelical Vision: The Presbyterian School and Emmanuel College / 16

3. The Return to Prince Albert: St. Alban's and All Saints Residential Schools / 34

4. On the Edge of the City: The Prince Albert Indian Residential School / 54

5. After the White Paper: The Prince Albert Student Residence / 85

6. Realizing a Vision: The Prince Albert Indian Student Education Centre / 95

7. Conclusions / 125

Bibliography / 128

Index / 131

Acknowledgments

I wish to thank the Prince Albert Grand Council (PAGC) and its Education Committee for granting me the opportunity to work on this project and for making the research findings available in book form to a larger audience both within and outside of the PAGC. Jerry McLeod, Peter Brook, Pat Cook and other members of the staff of the Prince Albert Indian Student Education Centre have provided tireless support and assistance while this book was researched and written. Cliff Star, Solomon Sanderson, Howard Bighead, Larry Goldade, Phyllis Eagle-Boadway and Velma Ermine kindly consented to be interviewed concerning various aspects of the history of residential schooling in Prince Albert.

The late Karen Marion provided valuable photographs of everyday life at PAISEC in the mid-1990s and also assisted in developing prints from older negatives held by the Prince Albert Historical Society. I thank Bill Smiley of the P.A. Historical Society, Mrs. Bernice Logan and the Anglican Diocese of Saskatchewan Archives for their permission to reproduce historical photographs pertaining to residential schooling in Prince Albert. Dan Gillis provided timely assistance in scanning some of these photographs, and Paul DeGrace kindly prepared the map. Donna Robertson quickly and ably prepared the index.

I am indebted to John Milloy for his generosity in discussing with me pertinent archival sources. George Brandak (Special Collections, University of British Columbia), Wilma Macdonald (National Archives of Canada), Wendy Ansell (Union of British Columbia Indian Chiefs), Jeff O'Brien (Archives of the Anglican Diocese of Saskatchewan), Stan Hanson (University of Saskatchewan Archives), and various staff members of the Saskatchewan Archives Board all provided much-appreciated assistance at various stages of the research.

Barbara Burnaby, Dara Culhane, Gerald Friesen, Philip Moore and Trefor Smith read earlier versions of this manuscript and offered many helpful suggestions and corrections. Zoë Dyck designed the book cover and assisted in the reproduction of some historical photographs, while other members of my family in Port Coquitlam, Ottawa and Saskatoon aided me in many other ways.

I thank all of the above for their generous contributions. Any shortcomings remaining in the book are mine alone.

List of Abbreviations

ADSA   Anglican Diocese of Saskatchewan Archives

CMS   Church Missionary Society (of the Church of England)

CSP   Canada Sessional Papers, Reports of the Department of Indian Affairs

DIAND   Department of Indian Affairs and Northern Development

ESL   English as a second language

FSI   Federation of Saskatchewan Indians (1958–early 1970s)

FSIN   Federation of Saskatchewan Indian Nations (since mid-1970s)

IAB   Indian Affairs Branch (mid-1930s–1960s)

ICFS   Indian Child and Family Services

INAC   Indian and Northern Affairs Canada

ISA   Indian Schools Administration (of the Missionary Society of the Church of England in Canada)

MSCC   Missionary Society of the Church of England in Canada

NAC   National Archives of Canada

PADC   Prince Albert District Chiefs (1970s–early 1980s)

PADCC   Prince Albert District Chiefs Council (mid-1980s–1992)

PAGC   Prince Albert Grand Council (since 1993)

PAISEC   Prince Albert Indian Student Education Centre (since 1985)

PASR   Prince Albert Student Residence (1969–1985)

PATC   Prince Albert Tribal Council (1992–1993)

PX   Records of the Prince Albert Indian Student Education Centre, PAGC

RSHD   Residential Schools and Hostel Division, of the MSCC (the successor to the ISA of the MSCC in the early 1960s)

RG10   Record Group 10 (NAC), Records of the Department of Indian Affairs

SAB   Saskatchewan Archives Board

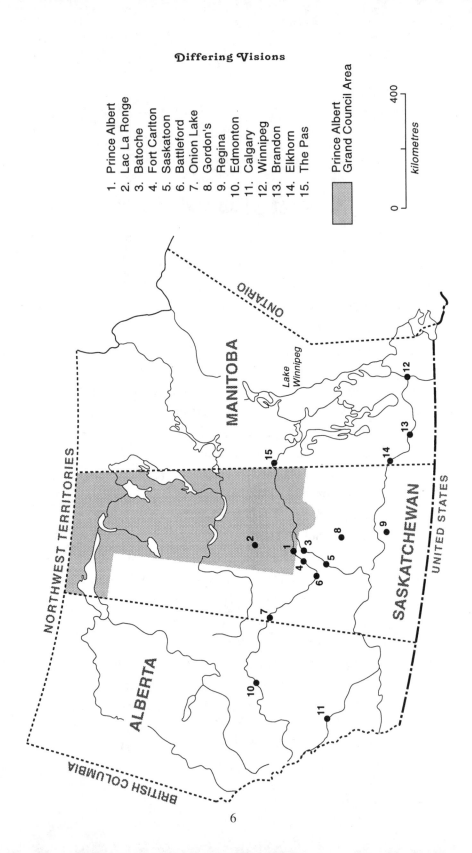

Differing Visions

1. Prince Albert
2. Lac La Ronge
3. Batoche
4. Fort Carlton
5. Saskatoon
6. Battleford
7. Onion Lake
8. Gordon's
9. Regina
10. Edmonton
11. Calgary
12. Winnipeg
13. Brandon
14. Elkhorn
15. The Pas

Prince Albert
Grand Council Area

kilometres

0   400

Foreword

by Grand Chief Alphonse Bird

Indian people in the Prince Albert Grand Council have long recognized the importance of education for our children. Our future as a people depends upon our ability to prepare our children to deal with a rapidly changing world that is not always sensitive to our need and determination to retain and build our culture and communities. To succeed in this it will be necessary to understand the often unhappy history of our relations with governments, religious denominations and other non-Indian agencies. Today some Canadians are in a rush to forget the past and to make Indians shoulder the responsibility for the serious difficulties that afflict our communities. This approach will not work. The past cannot be swept under the carpet and forgotten. Indians and non-Indians must deal honestly with the past as a first step towards finding ways to establish better tomorrows for all of us. We all stand to benefit from this.

This book tells the story of how residential schooling for Indian children has been administered in Prince Albert for more than a century. In some ways, our experience of residential schooling has been similar to that of other Aboriginal peoples throughout Canada and other countries. In other ways, however, our story is quite different. At a time when Indian residential schools were closing elsewhere in Canada, the people of the Prince Albert Grand Council saw a need to take over and completely remake an institution that had previously been used to direct and control our people. Recognizing the positive role that a completely different kind of Indian-controlled child education centre might play, we have created and pursued our own vision of how to care for and educate those of our children who require special treatment. The courage and commitment that our leaders and staff have shown in working to make this vision a reality deserves to be celebrated. The tactics that federal officials have employed to frustrate and undermine our efforts also need to be recorded.

This history has been written first and foremost for the Indian people of the Prince Albert Grand Council. The story needs to be told of how our ancestors, who signed treaties with the representatives of Queen Victoria, sought to obtain appropriate forms of education for their children, and how today we are carrying on that struggle. Moreover, we want to share our story with the people of Canada and other countries. Anyone who wishes to see the lives of Indian children

7

improved, but who may be uncertain about what needs to be done, can learn a great deal by studying how the federal government has actually dealt with an innovative and highly effective institution, built and operated by Indian people for Indian children. When we confront the past we learn how to build for the future.

Chapter 1

Introduction
The Significance of Indian Residential Schooling

The Purposes of This Study

This book examines the development of an innovative but little known under-taking in the field of residential schooling for First Nations children. Specifi-cally, it recounts the continuing efforts of Indian leaders and parents in north-central Saskatchewan to transform a residential school, originally constructed to foster the priorities of church and state, into an Indian-controlled institution that meets the particular needs of Indian children in a culturally effective manner. It is, in short, a story about how Aboriginal people have acted with courage and patient determination to reverse the sad effects of a history of stifling bureaucratic mismanagement of the education of their children.

The book identifies the different visions pursued over many decades by church and government officials on the one side, and by Indian parents and leaders on the other, concerning purposes and practices appropriate to residen-tial schooling for Indian children. The interpretation presented here is that the thorough-going refashioning of residential schooling, conducted since 1985 at the Prince Albert Indian Student Education Centre (PAISEC) by and for Indian people, demonstrates what can be accomplished through the practice of Indian self-government. PAISEC represents a signal achievement that deserves to be documented and celebrated, both inside and outside the band communities that comprise the Prince Albert Grand Council. Although PAISEC is scheduled to be closed after the summer of 1997, the struggle waged by Aboriginal people and the lessons they have learned in the process of turning what was once a traditional, church-operated, government-funded Indian residential school into a responsive, responsible and decidedly positive institution deserve to be remembered.

To appreciate not only the accomplishments registered by PAISEC during the past decade but also the circumstances that have dictated its closure, it is necessary to situate this distinctive institution within the long history of Indian residential schooling in this city, in Saskatchewan and in the country as a whole. In fact, Indian residential schooling commenced in Prince Albert a month after Canada became a nation in 1867 and has been conducted there for 93 of the subsequent 129 years. Following the Second World War the Prince Albert Indian Residential School emerged as the second largest institution of its type in Canada and eventually became the largest. The transformation of this institution from a church- and government-administered residence into a band-controlled educational and child development facility set the pace for similar developments elsewhere in Saskatchewan.

For better or for worse, the longstanding provision of Indian residential schooling in Prince Albert has contributed to shaping the childhood memories, family relations and educational experiences and opportunities of substantial numbers of Indian people over several generations. The complex and often controversial history of Indian residential schooling elsewhere in Canada has received much attention in recent years, as is evidenced by the growing number of publications by researchers and former pupils of these institutions. Major studies of the history and impact of Indian residential schools have been mounted by the Royal Commission on Aboriginal Peoples and the Assembly of First Nations, as well as tribal councils, religious denominations and scholars from a range of disciplines.[1] Court cases dealing with past instances of abuse suffered by students at residential schools have received substantial public attention. Notwithstanding these developments, the specific and somewhat unusual history of Indian residential schooling in Prince Albert did not receive systematic attention until the study that led to the writing of this book was commissioned by the Prince Albert Grand Council in 1994. The project was part of a larger review of the operations of the Prince Albert Indian Student Education Centre, an institution operated by the Grand Council on behalf of the twelve bands that make up the PAGC.

The history of residential schooling in Prince Albert has been distinctive in a number of respects. It began several years before the signing of treaties between the government of Canada and Indian nations in the Canadian west and well in advance of the development of federally-sponsored Indian schools in what would eventually become the prairie provinces. Previously, Indians in the Prince Albert area dealt directly with two Christian denominations in arranging voluntary residential schooling for Indian children at mission schools. This was followed in the early 1890s by a petition from several Indian chiefs to the federal government requesting support for a church-operated boarding school that would provide both academic and industrial training for Indian children. Emmanuel College, the Anglican boarding school that served Indian children from 1891 until 1908, was in some ways more sensitive to the wishes of Indian leaders and the needs of Indian children than were many other Indian residential schools (as is shown in the next chapter). Yet even at this early stage, federal officials were intransigent in their treatment of an educational institution that showed any inclination to compromise bureaucratic imperatives to accommodate Aboriginal parents' interests and concerns.

Two Anglican residential schools, temporarily relocated to Prince Albert during the 1940s, were eventually combined to establish a permanent Indian residential school in that city. While the operations of this school were in many respects similar to others in Canada, the physical form of the Prince Albert Indian Residential School was unlike that of most of its counterparts. Most significantly, however, residential schooling continued in Prince Albert after the 1960s and early 1970s closure of most other Indian residential schools in Canada. The experience of the Prince Albert Grand Council in working to create a new form of residential schooling—most often in the face of stubborn and less than principled resistance on the part of federal government officials—has not been a common element of the history of residential schooling outside Saskatchewan.

The primary objective of this study, therefore, has been to provide an account of the operational or administrative history of residential schooling for First Nations children in Prince Albert from the nineteenth century to 1995. Since few published accounts discuss in detail the operations of these successive local institutions, it has been necessary to conduct extensive documentary research in Prince Albert, Saskatoon, Ottawa and Vancouver. Most, but not all, of the existing archival and documentary records that pertain to Indian residential schooling in Prince Albert have been consulted, although certain files and records at the headquarters of the Department of Indian and Northern Affairs were not available for consultation when the research was carried out.[2] These materials would have to be examined to render more complete the account offered here.

It was decided at the outset of this study not to focus upon seeking out, recording and representing the personal memories and meanings that residential school attendance has held for a broad range of individual Indian students, families and communities. This decision was taken not because of any lack of interest in individuals' accounts but out of respect for the difficulty of accurately representing detailed, varied and highly personal memories by means of generalized statements and summary claims. In fact, I conducted a number of personal interviews that readily revealed the richness and significance of such information. Nevertheless, they remain the stories of these individuals, to be recounted when and as they wish. In due course, a more detailed and rounded understanding of the history of residential schooling in Prince Albert may result from combining the archivally-based analysis provided by this book with detailed accounts of personal experiences and memories of residential schooling by as many former pupils as possible. It would also be useful to consult parents, siblings and children of former pupils, staff members and band leaders whose lives and families have been touched directly or indirectly by the operations of residential schooling in Prince Albert. This larger task was simply beyond the mandate of the current project, although it is clearly a most worthwhile undertaking that the First Nations of the Prince Albert district may one day wish to address in their own way.

Accordingly, this account of the operational history of Indian residential schooling in Prince Albert seeks to provide an overview of the relevant programs and institutions that have operated in this city at different times since 1867. For the purposes of presentation, this history will be divided into five distinct institutional periods:

a) Presbyterian Mission School and Emmanuel College (1867–1908);

b) St. Alban's and All Saints Indian Residential Schools (1944–51);

c) Prince Albert Indian Residential School (1951–69);

d) Prince Albert Student Residence (1969–85); and

e) Prince Albert Indian Student Education Centre (1985–present).

The scope, format and organization of this book reflect the fact that it has been researched and written first and foremost for the people of the Prince Albert Grand Council. At the same time I recognize that the matters considered here may be of use to those who share an interest in the history of Indian residential schooling as well as in more general features of past and present relations between Aboriginal peoples and nation-states.

An Overview of Indian Administration and Residential Schooling in Canada

Before analyzing the administration of residential schools operated at different times in Prince Albert, it is important to note that here, as in other parts of the country, Indian residential schooling was from the outset shaped by a set of underlying political, economic and cultural relations between First Nations and the representatives of church and state.[3] The activities of early Christian missionaries who travelled to the Canadian west and north were financed and directed by various church organizations in eastern Canada, England and other parts of Europe. Their purposes were evangelical in nature, but were also informed by the prospect of future Euro-Canadian settlement of the Canadian west. The missionaries' self-appointed task of defining and ministering to what they believed to be the spiritual and social needs of Aboriginal peoples offered a means for ambitious denominations to establish local footholds and thereby prepare themselves to play prominent roles in the new communities expected to arise in the prairie west.

The interests of the Canadian state in dealing with Aboriginal peoples in western Canada were directly linked to the objectives of acquiring and opening these territories for Euro-Canadian settlement. Charged with the responsibility of building a new nation from sea to sea, federal officials recognized that the success of this project would depend in large part upon their ability to negotiate workable agreements or treaties with First Nations. The ill-fated attempt to transfer Rupert's Land and the North-West Territories from the Hudson's Bay Company to the Canadian government without first reaching agreement with Aboriginal peoples had sparked the Métis Rebellion of 1869–70 in Manitoba. Without mutually acceptable treaties it would be difficult to avoid the high costs of confrontation and military action that had characterized relations between Indian peoples and the American government. Thus, the transfer of land and other resources to the Crown and the subsequent settlement of western Canada rested in large part upon the ability of federal representatives to strike co-operative relations with Aboriginal peoples.

In the course of negotiating treaties with the federal government during the 1870s, Indian leaders sought to forge political and economic relationships that would recognize the rights and aspirations of their people within the new social order that was to be constructed on the lands they were prepared to share with the newcomers. Aboriginal people were well aware of the deep-seated ecological and social changes occurring in the prairie west. Thus, First Nations leaders insisted upon a series of treaty terms designed to assist their people in establishing acceptable new ways of life for themselves, their children and their grandchildren. The promise of government assistance to develop new livelihoods in the event of the disappearance of the buffalo was one key provision of Treaty Six. The provision of appropriate and useful forms of schooling was also identified by Indian leaders as an essential term. Thus, the signing of Treaty Six in 1876 not only surrendered to the Crown a vast territory across central Saskatchewan and Alberta, including the area around Prince Albert, but also marked the acceptance by government signatories of these negotiated commitments.

In the years following the signing of Treaty Six the disappearance of the buffalo from the Canadian plains led the Department of Indian Affairs to launch an agricultural development program along the lines anticipated in the terms of the treaty. Although the initial results of Indian farmers working under this program were promising, this brief period of partnership between federal officials and band communities was soon jeopardized by serious cutbacks in federal funding. The unrest created by these arbitrary measures brought together Indian leaders from across western Canada in a concerted attempt to oblige the federal government to live up to its treaty obligations (see Tobias 1983). But before this political initiative could be realized, hostilities between Métis residents and government forces broke out south of Prince Albert.

A Canadian military expedition to the North-West rapidly put down the 1885 Rebellion in a set of engagements that featured only limited involvement on the part of Indian people.[4] Nevertheless, the steps Indian leaders had previously taken to protest federal Indian policy, along with the unwarranted fear generated during the spring of 1885 by rumours of a possible large-scale Indian uprising, engendered an uncompromisingly authoritarian response from Ottawa. After the 1885 Rebellion the somewhat co-operative tenor of relations between Indian nations and the Canadian state withered as federal officials imposed a pattern of harsh and rigid administration by means of the Indian Act and other government regulations enacted without consultation with Indian communities. Moreover, by 1890, the commencement of substantial Euro-Canadian immigration into the prairie west had begun to render Aboriginal peoples a minority population within the region.

Adopting an approach that has been identified as "coercive tutelage,"[5] federal authorities began to act on the presumption that Indians did not know and perhaps could not know what was in their best interests, and would therefore need to be subjected to a regime of paternalism under which they would be stripped of civil, economic and cultural rights and subjected to bureaucratic direction. This racist perspective permeated the mandate of the Department of Indian Affairs to "solve" the so-called "Indian problem" and supported the operating assumption within federal government circles that Indians themselves were the source of the "problem." In consequence, federal Indian administration set out to rid Indians of their languages, cultures and social identities. A set of specialized institutions, administrative practices and regulations were created to transform Indians from members of Aboriginal cultures and communities into isolated individuals who could be readily assimilated into the new society with little or no lingering trace of their cultural ancestry.

Within this approach Indian schooling was engineered, first and foremost, to advance the objective of cultural assimilation. Since education was not defined as a federal power under the terms of the British North America Act (now known as the Constitution Act of 1867), federal officials opted to enlist the assistance of various churches in operating Indian schools, even though the administration of Indians and Indian lands was awarded to Ottawa. Subcontracting the running of Indian schools to religious denominations not only shored up the government's lack of expertise in this field, but was also favoured by federal officials as a means of informally off-loading some of the costs onto the churches. Although the rhetoric of federal Indian administration characteristically implied nothing less than total commitment to the objective of assimilation, in practice the Department of Indian Affairs was almost never provided with sufficient funds to meet its mandate. In consequence, the church-operated Indian schools suffered from chronic underfunding.

In addition to establishing some relatively inexpensive day schools on reserves, the federal government initiated church-operated industrial schools (in off-reserve locations) and boarding schools (usually located on or near reserves) to which Indian children could be removed to "protect" them from the supposedly backward and deleterious influence of their parents and families. In time the distinction between the vocationally-oriented industrial schools and the typically less well-equipped boarding schools became moot, and in official correspondence both came to be referred to simply as "residential schools."

The residential school was the key institution for promoting assimilation. It was designed to separate Indian children from their families so they could be systematically fitted with the religious beliefs, social habits and educational training that would turn them into "brown white men." This task of making Indian children different than and ashamed of their parents may have been cast in moral terms as being in the best interests of the children, but it nevertheless relied upon the power that federal authorities could exercise over the everyday lives of Indian families and communities. However, this power was never absolute. Indians developed many means for resisting the coercive tutelage to which they were subjected. Indian parents sought to do the best they could for their children under very difficult circumstances. Although they had quite different aspirations for their children than did officers of the Department of Indian Affairs, Indian communities did not deny the possible utility of formal educational training within Canadian society. Instead, they sought to discover ways of acquiring positive educational opportunities for their children without surrendering to the demeaning presumption that educated Indians would surely want to separate themselves from their families and cultures.

This history of residential schooling for Indian children in Prince Albert seeks not only to focus upon the policies and purposes of missionaries and federal officials but to highlight the sustained efforts of Indian communities to pursue their own goals. It is by no means a history of an equal and open partnership between bands and government and church authorities. Nevertheless, it does speak to more than a century of unflagging determination on the part of Indian people to survive the worst features of church- and government-operated residential schooling while working to build an educational institution that would meet some of their children's needs. Nor has their struggle ended. The political processes and differing visions described and analyzed in this book cannot be readily consigned to a distant history of long-abandoned forms of Indian administration. The relationships and forces that figure in this story reach from the nineteenth century to the present day.

Notes

1. See, for example, the following publications, which represent only a small portion of the recently published literature on Indian residential schooling in Canada: Assembly of First Nations 1994; Canadian Conference of Catholic Bishops 1995; Furniss 1995; Haig-Brown 1988; Jaine 1993; Logan 1993; Miller 1996; Nock 1988. John Milloy's study of residential schooling conducted for the Royal Commission on Aboriginal Peoples should be forthcoming shortly.
2. These INAC files seem likely to contain material dating back to the operation of the Prince Albert Indian Residential School by the Anglican Church during the 1960s and perhaps even earlier.
3. For a general history of the Canadian prairies, see Friesen 1987. For histories of Anglican and Roman Catholic mission work in Western Canada see, respectively, Boon 1962 and Choquette 1995.
4. Few if any members of bands belonging to what is today the Prince Albert Grand Council took an active part in the rebellion.
5. For a full account of the application of coercive tutelage within Canadian Indian administration and of the resistance that it engendered among Indians, see Dyck 1991.

Chapter 2

The Evangelical Vision

The Presbyterian School and Emmanuel College

Setting the Scene

The history of Indian residential schooling is inextricably rooted in the sweeping changes that transformed the prairie west in the last half of the nineteenth century. Within a few short decades a vast territory that once sustained a remarkably affluent Aboriginal hunting and fur trade economy experienced an irreversible ecological and economic shift to agriculture and other pursuits. The huge area that the Canadian government nominally purchased from the Hudson's Bay Company in 1870 was formally surrendered by First Nations through a series of treaties concluded with the Crown later in that decade. The disappearance of the buffalo from the Canadian plains in the late 1870s was quickly followed by the mounting of a reserve agricultural program and then the 1885 Rebellion. Twenty years later the prairie west had been divided into the provinces of Manitoba, Saskatchewan and Alberta. Countless newly created settlements sprouted into rural municipalities, towns and cities that attracted hundreds of thousands of non-Aboriginal settlers from eastern Canada, the United States and Europe. Telegraph lines, railroads and a burgeoning network of roads crisscrossed lands that had long been the traditional hunting territories of Aboriginal peoples.

Indian residential schooling evolved in Prince Albert throughout this period. Indeed, the establishment of Prince Albert as a settlement in the 1860s was part of a missionary initiative that sought to bring residential schooling and the Christian faith to Aboriginal people. Nevertheless, between 1867 and 1908 Prince Albert grew from a small mission located in the midst of Cree country into the major administrative centre for northern Saskatchewan. What was more, Indian residential schooling would come to play a telling role in the development of Prince Albert as an urban centre and in the efforts of First Nations people in north-central Saskatchewan to respond to the forces that had reshaped their political, economic and cultural surroundings.

The Nisbet Mission

The founding of a Presbyterian mission on the banks of the North Saskatchewan River[1] by the Reverend James Nisbet in July 1866 marked the beginning of the future City of Prince Albert as well as the commencement of residential schooling for Indian children within that community. Nisbet met with local Cree almost immediately upon his arrival:

> Providentially the principal Indians belonging to the place were camped within two miles of where we purposed [sic] to establish our camp, so no time was lost in conferring with them about their willingness that we should remain among them. Our consultations with them extended over two days. I need not repeat all that passed between us during these two anxious days. It is sufficient to say that—with the blessing of God—all their scruples were removed and they unanimously agreed that we should be allowed to remain and carry on the work to which we have been appointed. (Nisbet 1869:2)

One of Nisbet's priorities was to create a school where Indian children would be taught "the arts of civilised life, together with the ordinary branches of a Christian education" (Nisbet 1869:1). Nisbet began offering lessons informally to Indian children shortly after his arrival, and by May 1867 five Indian children had been left by their parents to live with him and his family while they received schooling (Nisbet 1869:6).

A regular school was created at the Presbyterian Mission towards the end of that summer, and a teacher was hired to teach Indian as well as Métis children the basics of reading, writing and arithmetic, as well as geography, history, English composition and bookkeeping[2]. Although lessons were initially conducted in English, some instruction in Cree was added by the third year of the school's operation. During the first two years some fourteen native children spent longer or shorter periods living at the mission and attending the school[3]. Nisbet reported that "[t]wo of these have been removed by death, and others have gone or have been taken away from other causes, chiefly on account of their wishing to be with their parents" (1869:6). By 1872 a total of eighteen Indian and twenty-two Métis children had attended the mission school (Oliver 1934:71).

Nonetheless, Nisbet's efforts to establish a school and a farm that would make the mission self-sufficient did not satisfy his superiors' expectations. Letters from church authorities repeatedly urged him to spend less time at the mission so that he might travel through the countryside contacting Indian bands and seeking converts to Christianity rather than waiting for them to come to him. Nisbet's unwillingness to adopt this course of action eventually led to an inquiry into the operation of the mission by the Foreign Mission Committee of the Presbyterian Church. After visiting Prince Albert in the fall of 1872, the Rev. William Moore reported that, according to Nisbet's own standards and objectives, the mission had been highly successful. Yet the evangelical purposes of the church would, Moore recommended, be better served by abandoning the mission farm and travelling out of the settlement to preach the Gospel.[4]

The publication of Moore's report in 1873 deeply offended Nisbet, prompting him and his family to leave Prince Albert the following year.[5] Thereafter the mission and the Presbyterian school in Prince Albert began to focus less upon dealing with Indians in the settlement and more upon Scottish and Métis settlers arriving from Manitoba. After 1881 the Presbyterian Church in Prince Albert largely gave up mission work with Indians in Prince Albert (Grant 1984:153), although its work on reserves continued. While the Presbyterian school in Prince Albert carried on, it now served primarily as a day school for the children of local settlers.[6]

Transitions and Treaty-Making

The consecration of the first Bishop of Saskatchewan by the Church of England in 1874 happened to coincide with Rev. Nisbet's departure from Prince Albert. Arriving at Prince Albert for the first time early in 1875, Bishop McLean brought with him an enthusiasm for evangelism, an academic background and previous teaching experience at St. John's College in Manitoba. During his twelve years service as Bishop of Saskatchewan he travelled widely within the diocese, from Lake Winnipeg to the Rocky Mountains, and visited Eastern Canada and England on several occasions to raise funds to support the expansion of the Anglican Church within the Diocese of Saskatchewan, the administrative centre of which was located in Prince Albert. The "Indian work," as it was called in Anglican correspondence, was to be a key component of the overall operations of the Diocese of Saskatchewan during the remainder of the nineteenth century.

From the perspective of Bishop McLean and other non-Aboriginal settlers, the events of the 1870s and 1880s represented a period of promise and opportunity, for they envisioned themselves as pioneers building a new country that they hoped would soon become heavily populated and prosperous. For Aboriginal peoples this period was one of ecological catastrophe during which the buffalo rapidly disappeared, leaving those who had depended upon the bison to search for new ways to support themselves. In response to the ecological, political and social forces being exerted upon their lands and ways of life, Indian bands sought to establish formal relations with the Crown and working partnerships with government and church agencies to facilitate the development of new forms of subsistence, which would in turn sustain their families, cultures and communities. Accordingly, the Indians of Western Canada negotiated a series of treaties with the federal government during the 1870s. The provision of schooling to Indian children was one of the terms insisted upon by the Indian leaders who negotiated Treaty Six in 1876 (Morris 1880:184, 217, 353).

The manner in which this particular treaty commitment came to be interpreted by federal authorities had much in common with the way in which the Department of Indian Affairs managed a broader treaty commitment to assist Indians in taking up farming and new forms of livelihood[7]. In the wake of the sudden disappearance of the buffalo from the Canadian plains in 1878 and 1879, the federal government initiated a reserve agricultural policy that aimed to help new Indian farmers to become self-sufficient within a few years. Although federal support for this undertaking was driven by a desire to reduce the sums of money being spent on rationing Indians who had suddenly been rendered unable to feed themselves, there initially developed a relatively workable form of partnership between some employees of the department and many new Indian farmers, both of whom were working towards a common goal. These promising working relationships were fueled by the determination of Indian bands to regain their economic autonomy as quickly as possible.

However, the early success of this initiative and the overall tenor of dealings between Indian nations and the federal government were undermined by an economic recession that prompted Ottawa to slash expenditures within the field of Indian affairs, notwithstanding its treaty commitments. These cutbacks transformed the sense of co-operation that had started to develop between some bands and some officers of the Department of Indian Affairs. Reductions in government spending ignited a feeling of mistrust that contributed to a basic reshaping of relations between Indians and the state, relationships that were eroded even more by the events of 1885. Although Indian participation in the 1885 Rebellion was limited, it provoked an extreme and lasting reaction within the Department of Indian Affairs. Any previous commitment to the principle of working *with* Indians within federal circles was replaced by an authoritarian stance that declared Indians incapable of knowing what was in their best interests and, therefore, forced them to submit to the will and wisdom of the state. Thereafter, the Department of Indian Affairs was charged with exercising control over most aspects of everyday life in Indian communities in order to facilitate the assimilation of Indians into Canadian society. Under this new regime, Canadian Indian administration came to constitute an ongoing program of coercive tutelage which, through the operations of the Department of Indian Affairs as well as those of Christian denominations that came to play a leading role in Indian education, served to shape the experience of succeeding generations of Indians.

The Creation of Emmanuel College
The history of Indian residential schooling in Prince Albert up to and including the first decade of the twentieth century exhibited elements of both co-operation and friction in dealings among Indians, the federal government and the Anglican Church. But the development of Anglican residential schooling for Indians was also impelled by a plan within the Church of England to render it one of the leading denominations in the new society developing on the northern plains.

Upon his arrival in the sprawling Prince Albert settlement in 1875, Bishop McLean oversaw the construction of St. Mary's Church and a house for himself and his family. During his tenure as Bishop of Saskatchewan he collected nearly $90,000 in cash from Anglican benefactors in Eastern Canada and Great Britain,[8] in addition to the contribution of river lots upon which St. Mary's and later Emmanuel College were constructed. These funds and lands were invested to create an institutional infrastructure to aid the efforts of the Anglican Church in Saskatchewan both in pursuing converts within band communities and in claiming the adherence of incoming settlers.

Recognizing that the "Indian work" could provide a viable basis for attracting financial contributions to the diocese, McLean drafted a plan to create a theological college in Prince Albert to train native and non-native catechists, lay readers, missionaries and priests who could be sent forth to seek converts and to build Anglican congregations. This institution, which he named Emmanuel College, opened in temporary quarters in November 1879, making use of books sent from Cambridge University. The first class of men included five Indians, two Métis and four men of European heritage, all of whom studied English, theology and the grammar and composition of Cree.[9] The courses were taught mostly by Bishop McLean and Archdeacon John Mackay, the son of a Hudson's Bay Company officer who had spoken Cree from childhood and had served as one of the interpreters during the negotiation of Treaty Six.

The creation of Emmanuel College fit within the guidelines of an Anglican evangelical strategy known as the "Native Church Policy."[10] Under this policy Anglican missionaries working with native peoples were expected to make the development of a native clergy one of their first priorities. This approach anticipated that Aboriginal people could, through the timely provision of appropriate assistance, construct self-governing, self-financing and self-propagating native congregations, thereby freeing non-Aboriginal missionaries and funding to pursue new evangelical endeavours in other fields. This policy, unlike others adopted by churches and governments in later years, placed as much or more emphasis upon working with Aboriginal adults and communities as with Aboriginal children. What this meant was that adults were not considered to be members of a "lost generation" who could not profitably be worked with or who were beyond redemption. Because Aboriginal adults were seen as being capable persons, there was little impetus to focus exclusively upon children or to insist upon removing or "rescuing" them from the supposedly deleterious influence of their families and communities. While the Native Church Policy certainly aimed to convert Aboriginal people to Christianity, promote education and encourage Indians to change their ways of life, this policy did not doubt the ability of native peoples to regain their independence and be self-supporting. In consequence, while the provision of formal schooling was seen as being beneficial to Indian children and their communities, it was not deemed essential to keep Indian boys and girls apart from their parents or to insulate them from their communities.

A year after its commencement Emmanuel College moved into a set of buildings (including residence facilities) specially constructed for this purpose near St. Mary's Church, a few miles west of the Presbyterian Mission. The funds expended on providing suitable accommodation for the college represented a substantial investment of the capital raised by Bishop McLean, and the opening of the new college buildings was a major social event attended by prominent figures from across the North-West Territories. It was anticipated that these facilities would become a focal feature of not only the Prince Albert settlement but, indeed, the Territories as a whole. By 1881, when the Governor General of Canada visited Emmanuel College, a high school for the fee-paying sons of settlers had been added to the facilities, but the main work remained that of theological training to provide the personnel needed to build congregations throughout the diocese. Bishop McLean also hoped one day to establish an agricultural demonstration farm on the property where Indian men could be taught the essentials of agriculture in a more effective manner than had been possible through the underfunded federal reserve agricultural program. In 1883 McLean's dreams reached a high point when he obtained a charter to create the University of Saskatchewan, of which Emmanuel College was to be a key element (see Murray 1956). In his address to the Synod of the Diocese of Saskatchewan in August 1886, Bishop McLean outlined his vision for the future:

> I am making arrangements for carrying on the work of Indian training at Emmanuel College on a much larger scale than has hitherto been attempted. Up to this time the Indian students have been in training only for mission work, and their number has therefore been necessarily very limited. It is now proposed to train as large a number of Indians as possible, not only in the composition of their own language, and in the ordinary English branches, but in the elements of chemistry, especially in its application to farming or agriculture. The college possesses a very good chemical laboratory which I brought over from England and Germany, and during the past term lectures on chemistry and its application to agriculture, have been delivered daily with experiments. The pupils are taught how plants grow—what substances in the soil and atmosphere form their food—how different kinds of crops withdraw from the soil different constituents . . . . The college possesses 200 acres of the best farming land. A part of it is being prepared for farming and gardening, that the pupils may have practical outdoor training in addition to that of the classroom. Indians will be trained in this way, with the view, in some cases, of their becoming intelligent farmers, and in others acting as schoolmasters to Indian children on the reserves. I had the gratification a few weeks ago of

appointing, at the request of the Indian department, one of our Indian students to be teacher of a government Indian school. He has had training in English branches for three college terms, and a few months training in agricultural chemistry.[11]

However, McLean's lofty aspirations for Emmanuel College were not to be realized for several reasons. First, the 1885 Rebellion began to transform the nature of Indian administration in Western Canada. The authoritarian policies and practices adopted by federal officials thereafter had the effect of stripping Indians of autonomy, defining them as incapable of knowing what was in their best interests and subjecting them to programs of forced assimilation. Second, the English-based Church Missionary Society, which had supported Emmanuel College's work with and for Aboriginal peoples, announced that it would be withdrawing its financial contributions to this and other Canadian Anglican missions over a period of years. Third, the town and later the city of Prince Albert ended up developing around the site of the original Presbyterian Mission, leaving the site of Emmanuel College several miles out of town. When the Presbyterian School in Prince Albert added a collegiate or high school class in 1885, enrolment at the Emmanuel College Collegiate School declined sharply, notwithstanding the significant investment that had been put into the college buildings and facilities. Finally, the death of Bishop McLean three months after his address to the synod left Emmanuel College without his able and determined leadership.

𝔉rom 𝔘niversity to 𝔍ndian ℜesidential 𝔖chool

The next Bishop of Saskatchewan viewed Emmanuel College as being ahead of its time in terms of the requirements of the country and beyond the financial capacities of the Diocese of Saskatchewan, even though the college had been debt-free at the time of Bishop McLean's death. To finance the continuing operation and upkeep of the campus facility, application was made to the Department of Indian Affairs to have it funded as a boarding school for Indian children. Approval and initial funding was received in 1890, the same year in which a petition was submitted by several chiefs in the Prince Albert area to have not merely a boarding school but a full industrial school located in Prince Albert so that their children would not be obliged to attend the Battleford Industrial School. The support of Chiefs James Smith, John Smith, Mistawasis and Starblanket reflected their active involvement in the synod deliberations of the Diocese of Saskatchewan and a powerful desire among Indians to have children attend school closer to home and so be readily visited by parents in the event of illness.[12] The history of Emmanuel College's dealings with Indians up to that point had been relatively positive and co-operative in nature compared to those then emerging between reserve residents and employees of the Department of Indian Affairs. Indeed, throughout its eighteen years of operation as an Indian boarding school, Emmanuel College seemed to enjoy a measure of support from and respect for Indian leaders that permitted this institution to avoid some, though by no means all, of the serious problems that plagued the operation of other industrial, boarding and residential schools in Western Canada.[13]

The first federally-funded industrial school for Indian children in Western Canada had been opened in Battleford in 1883. After 1885 the Department of Indian Affairs' education policy increasingly favoured the removal of Indian children to church-administered industrial and boarding schools where their language and culture could be systematically removed and replaced by behaviours and beliefs calculated to turn them into "civilized" beings quite unlike their parents. By 1890 government policy firmly favoured residential schooling over reserve day schools as the most effective means for eliminating the so-called "Indian problem."

The continuing interest that Indian leaders and parents took in the operations of Emmanuel College, in spite of the manner in which federal policy systematically sought to discourage their participation in the schooling of their children, flatly contradicted the fundamental assumptions of government thinking. Indian leaders were firm in their determination to influence the administration of Emmanuel College, and their efforts seem to have had a beneficial impact upon the operation of this particular institution. The fact that this residential school did not employ corporal punishment to discipline its pupils was commented upon over the years by inspectors and visitors. That the first principal of this boarding school, Archdeacon John Mackay, could speak Cree fluently and, just as important, was willing to converse with pupils in their own language were distinctive features of Emmanuel College.[14] Therefore, although Emmanuel College was obliged to take note of the policies and instructions of the Department of Indian Affairs as a condition of receiving government funding, its operations never entirely corresponded with the strident tone of federal policy that envisioned Indian children as passive recipients of residential schooling and their parents as entirely out of the picture. Emmanuel College seems to have remained more responsive to, respectful of and in touch with Indian people than other residential schools.

The initial grant made by the Department of Indian Affairs to Emmanuel College provided for the schooling of ten boys at $100 per capita. This "pupilage" (i.e., the number of pupils who would be funded by the federal government) was increased to twenty by 1892, and the college argued that it should not be required to provide manual training in a broad range of trades since it was intended to serve as a sort of normal school that would prepare Indian children to teach in reserve communities.[15] In this way as in others, Emmanuel College remained unlike other government-subsidized boarding schools. Although boarding schools were typically located on or near Indian reserves, Emmanuel College was located adjacent to a settlement that would soon become a city. Moreover, while not designated as an industrial school, Emmanuel

College was initially distinguished from other residential facilities by virtue of its past involvement in developing Indian teachers and the hope that it would continue to do so. In any event, by the fall of 1895 the pupilage had been increased to a total of thirty in order to permit ten girls to attend Emmanuel College in addition to the twenty boys already provided for. In practice, the actual number of pupils attending the school at any given time often exceeded the number that the Department of Indian Affairs funded since non-status native children were from time to time permitted by church officials to attend the school.

In 1895, everyday life for pupils at Emmanuel College featured a full schedule of studies and chores:

> The regular routine is: study from 7.30 a.m. in summer and 8 in winter to 8.30 when the bell rings for breakfast. After breakfast the beds are made and rooms swept, and there is a short time for recreation. School opens at 9.30 and closes at 12. Dinner at 12.30 and school again at 1.30 to 3 p.m. From 3 to 4 p.m. the pupils are at work getting wood and water, sweeping and tidying the rooms again and working in the stables or carpenter's shop. There is study again from 7 to 8.15 pm.

> All the work on the premises is done by the pupils, and the boys who milk the cows and attend the stables have to do this work so as not to interfere with the studies and class work.

> [The girls] . . . attend classes regularly with the boys, and are also taught sewing, knitting, cooking and general housework.[16]

The school adopted decidedly less strict practices in its treatment of Indian boys and girls than federal officials would have preferred. For instance, the Deputy Superintendent General of Indian Affairs complained to the Indian Affairs minister that Principal Mackay openly disputed the department's contention that it was better to keep children "as far from parents as possible."[17] The deputy argued, nonetheless, that the experience of the department was considerably wider than Mackay's in dealing with Indians: "his assertion that not a pupil who has been given leave from Emmanuel College to visit his parents failed to return by no means disproves that the constant visiting of parents and friends . . . disturbs the pupils and gives opportunity for communication which has a retarding influence."[18] Clearly, Mackay had greater respect for and better relations with Indian parents than did senior officials of the Department of Indian Affairs. Moreover, government officials who visited Emmanuel College remarked upon the "excellent progress" being made by pupils in a range of academic subjects including the English language, reading, writing, geography, history, arithmetic, general knowledge, recitations, vocal and instrumental music and religious instruction.[19]

One problem that plagued Emmanuel College as well as other boarding and industrial schools during that period was the spread of tuberculosis and other highly infectious diseases. By 1896 several deaths among pupils at Emmanuel College sparked complaints from relatives that prompted the setting up of a commission of inquiry by the Diocese of Saskatchewan. After meeting with parents and some students, the commission reported its regret concerning the deaths but concluded that the college was not operating inappropriately. Indeed, earlier requests from Principal Mackay to the department for financial assistance to treat the increasing number of tuberculosis patients had encountered resistance from officials in Ottawa.[20] Eventually funding for this purpose was grudgingly granted, but in general the federal government sought to operate residential schools as inexpensively as possible.

Federal inspectors who visited Emmanuel College identified needed improvements, including hiring an additional teacher, improving the facility's ventilation system, and supplying more equipment, books and children's furniture.[21] These necessities, however, required additional funding and Ottawa remained unwilling to further subsidize Emmanuel College or any other boarding or industrial school for Indian children. In consequence, schools like Emmanuel College were obliged to seek authorization to increase the number of pupils since the federal government stubbornly resisted raising the size of per capita grants. By 1897 the department had increased the pupilage of Emmanuel to sixty but refused to permit the college to fund the cost of renovating or constructing buildings out of these funds.[22] Since these buildings were not government property, argued departmental officials, church authorities could decide at any moment to use these for purposes other than operating Indian schools. While not prepared to fund the full cost of operating residential schools, the Department of Indian Affairs continued to proclaim the need for industrial and boarding schools and to subcontract their management to the churches:

> The Department has fully recognized its inability to conduct [boarding and industrial schools] . . . as economically as can be done by denominations, and consequently it has endeavoured to have their management placed in the hands of the respective churches interested in them.[23]

Federal officials were well aware that the inadequacy of the grants offered to the schools would oblige these institutions to meet shortages from outside sources. Nevertheless, it called upon the churches to operate schools that would not only educate Indian children but transform them as individuals. The annual report of the Department of Indian Affairs for 1896 even advocated the involvement of government and church personnel in arranging "suitable" marriages among graduates of residential schools so that these young Indian men and women could be influenced to avoid "reverting to the old mode of living" from which they had been taken.

The Displeasure of the Department

The difficulties Emmanuel College encountered with respect to the policy guidelines and moral injunctions set for residential schooling by Ottawa were compounded by the systematic underfunding of schooling operations. The tensions thus created came to a head early in the new century, shortly after Rev. J.A. Mackay stepped down as principal and was replaced by Rev. James Taylor.[24] In reviewing the operations of the Indian boarding school, Taylor discovered that its pupilage had been arbitrarily reduced by departmental officials. For more than a year Taylor sought to restore the school's pupilage to sixty to obtain an increased per capita grant that would equal the funding provided to industrial schools,[25] and to secure funds to build a new boys' dormitory. The new principal also put much effort into expanding the farm operated by pupils at the college so that the produce grown would reduce the cost of feeding the pupils. Taylor's arguments encountered a veritable brick wall in Ottawa. Suddenly the operations of Emmanuel College were subjected to detailed and lengthy criticisms by government personnel, although there is no evidence that the school had changed much from previous years when it had been judged to be "excellent."

In a letter to the Indian Commissioner concerning the government's refusal to provide sufficient funding to Emmanuel College because, as federal officials argued, the funding of residential schools had not been a treaty commitment, Taylor replied:

> I agree with you when you say, "nothing was said [in the treaties] about institutions where pupils would be fed and clothed, etc." On the other hand nothing was said about the appointment of a Superintendent General of Indian Affairs, an Indian Commissioner, Inspectors and other highly salaried officials. All this came afterwards, and I am not for a moment questioning the wisdom of what has in these ways been done by Parliament and the Government of the day. But I am sure that the idea and spirit of the treaties was that the greatest benefits possible should accrue to our Indians.[26]

In making these comments Taylor tapped into a set of claims about the spirit of the treaties that had been developed by Cree leaders since the 1880s. Although Taylor endeavoured to apply these claims to support the specific requirements of Emmanuel College, his familiarity with these themes suggests that he had discussed these matters in some detail with Cree leaders who had not only taken part in the negotiation of Treaty Six but had also participated in the governance of the Diocese of Saskatchewan since the 1880s.

Taylor's arguments enraged federal officials who thereafter took every opportunity to find fault with Emmanuel College. When Taylor inquired why the Duck Lake Boarding School operated by the Roman Catholics received a higher per capita grant per pupil than did his school, departmental officials stated that "Emmanuel College has never been any other than a very ordinary boarding school" and maintained that Duck Lake offered a wider range of trades training that put it almost on a par with industrial schools.[27] Officers of the department also gave short shrift to evidence that Emmanuel College had succeeded as an Indian teacher training college by preparing at least seven of its graduates to become teachers in Indian day schools on reserves and sending two of its graduates to attend theological college in Toronto. The distinctive character and purposes of Emmanuel College were simply out of keeping with the government's program to pursue "de-tribalization"[28] and transform Indians from members of autonomous cultures and communities into individuals who had been stripped of their cultures and communal relationships. The federal government was less interested in producing qualified Indian school teachers than it was in forcing band members to become independent small-scale farmers and labourers who could be readily assimilated into Canadian society. Adopting a stance that would be replicated by their successors on several occasions in the coming century (including during the 1990s), federal officials were only too ready to force a school that had shown some responsiveness to Indian concerns to shift its priorities to suit bureaucratic priorities. Whatever the cost to Indian children, the bureaucratic preference for absolute conformity and standardization of residential school operations was to be upheld.

The priority placed upon agricultural and trades training within federal Indian education policy prompted Taylor to de-emphasize the academic components of the school's curriculum and to expand the scope of the farm and gardening activities carried out by the pupils at Emmanuel College,[29] although this move also helped to reduce the costs of feeding the boys and girls at the school. In 1903 the school introduced the half-day system of education under which pupils spent considerably less time in the classroom than had previously been the case at Emmanuel College.[30] Later that year Taylor travelled to Ottawa to press the case for additional funding for the school. He produced records to show that the school had been incurring debt in recent years and that government commitments to assist in the upkeep of the college's buildings had not been fully honoured.[31] Taylor skillfully gathered support from the bishop, the local member of Parliament and Prince Albert businessmen for increased government funding for the school. By 1905, when the school's accumulated debt had reached $8,000 and bank officials who had studied the records of Emmanuel College concluded that the debt had not resulted from extravagant spending by Taylor,[32] federal authorities finally relented and reluctantly paid off the deficit.[33] The department flatly refused, however, to provide funds for new buildings, which were by all accounts badly needed to provide more sanitary conditions for the students.

Infectious diseases continued to be as serious a problem at Emmanuel College as in most other residential schools during this period. In 1895 one girl died at the school while three other pupils had been sent home ill. In 1900 a pupil died after being returned home to the John Smith Reserve. A measles epidemic swept through the school in 1902 confining forty-two children to their beds and quarantining the school for a month; four children subsequently died.[34] The following year scarlet fever struck the school, resulting in a seven-week quarantine; that year there were also cases of acute bronchitis and pneumonia, yet all but one pupil recovered. A physician hired by the department to attend to the pupils advised that the boys' dormitory could not be made a healthy building,[35] but the department claimed to be unable to provide funds to replace it. A few months later the same physician resigned in a dispute with the department over payment for his services. A year later a new physician hired by the department to attend to Emmanuel College produced a list of pupils suffering from tuberculosis and scrofula. While indicating that these children could be successfully treated, he was not prepared to do so for the level of compensation offered by the department.[36] Another pupil died at the college in 1905, and a teacher died of pleurisy the next year. Once again Taylor went to Ottawa seeking funding for a new boys' dormitory, and once again his request was refused.

In 1907 P.H. Bryce, the medical officer for the Department of Indian Affairs, was commissioned to study the medical status of pupils and the sanitary conditions at boarding and industrial schools for Indians in Western Canada. Bryce's report summarized the alarming mortality rates among pupils that had been experienced in residential schools across the west,[37] noting that the department's per capita grant funding formula had essentially encouraged many schools to enroll and retain sickly children in order to maintain the size of their grants. The subsequent publication of the report caused widespread criticism of the overall operations of the Department of Indian Affairs in general and of residential schools in particular. Although the report noted that six pupils had been discharged from Emmanuel College the previous year due to poor health, none of the children present at the school when Bryce had inspected it had been "tuberculorized."[38] Nonetheless, the findings of the Bryce Report provided additional impetus within government to rethink the residential schooling program and to identify particular institutions that might be closed in order to reduce the required level of government funding.

The Closure of Emmanuel College

Although Emmanuel College was by no means the least healthy of the schools reviewed in Bryce's report, federal officials opportunistically made tactical use of this document in their dealings with the school.[39] Taylor's demand that the federal government ought to provide Indians with suitable residential schooling by virtue of the treaties was simply unacceptable to Ottawa. Moreover, the failure of Emmanuel College to implement departmental directives to keep children away from their parents had never been appreciated within the federal bureaucracy. When Emmanuel College began to claim once again that it was incurring a debt through its operations, the Department of Indian Affairs steadfastly refused to provide any additional support. Over a period of approximately a year and a half a variety of proposals seeking to retain Emmanuel College were sent to Ottawa, but in the end the federal government, with the support of a key Anglican layman in Toronto, refused to make available the required funding. Petitions signed by Indian parents in support of retaining the school were forwarded to Ottawa to no avail.[40] Thus, at the end of June 1908, the boarding school at Emmanuel College was closed as a part of a larger set of residential school closures. In the following days its students were either returned home to attend reserve day schools or sent to the Battleford Industrial School.[41]

Although Rev. Taylor had never wavered in his support of the boarding school at Emmanuel College, there is evidence that the Church as a whole had a number of other interests that were not jeopardized by the closure of this institution. In 1906 Archdeacon Lloyd had re-established an Anglican theological college in Prince Albert, at which time some of the endowed funding from the Diocese of Saskatchewan that had paid part of Taylor's salary was reallocated to Lloyd. Subsequently the Charter for the University of Saskatchewan, which had been granted to Emmanuel College during the time of Bishop McLean, was surrendered so that a provincial university with this name could be established in Saskatoon. In the fall of 1909 the revived theological college was removed from Prince Albert to Saskatoon, where it became one of the founding colleges of the new University of Saskatchewan.

The interests of the Anglican Church with respect to Indian residential schooling in the Diocese of Saskatchewan had also been maintained through the construction of boarding schools under its control at Onion Lake in the western part of the province and at Lac la Ronge in 1907.[42] The two river lots the Diocese of Saskatchewan had acquired many years before, and upon one of which Emmanuel College had been constructed, did not in the end turn out to be bad investments for the diocese, even though their value had temporarily diminished when the City of Prince Albert developed its centre several miles east of where McLean had expected. In 1906 the Bishop of Saskatchewan was asked to sell one of these lots to the Department of Justice for the purposes of creating a federal penitentiary,[43] and for a while he pondered the possibility of selling and continuing to operate a boarding school for Indians on the neighbouring lot. Yet in the end both lots were sold by the diocese and became the site for Saskatchewan's federal penitentiary. What had been the site of an innovative approach to Indian residential schooling came to be used for quite different purposes. With the sale of these lands the Diocese of Saskatchewan offset the cost of constructing St. Alban's Ladies College, a residential school for fee-paying girls situated on Central Avenue in Prince Albert. In the end, the Diocese of Saskatchewan did not lose any capital assets following the collapse of its ambitious theological college and boys' college in the late 1880s.[44] The use of these facilities for housing a boarding school for Indian pupils between 1890 and 1908 provided a means of keeping Emmanuel College alive and functioning both as an institutional entity and as a physical facility when it would have otherwise been disposed of for a considerably smaller return than in 1908.

What had been lost was a residential school initiative that, whatever its failings, had endeavoured to educate Indian children without entirely succumbing to the fundamentally racist assumptions enshrined within federal educational policy during this era. The report of the principal of Emmanuel College for 1903 ended with the following statement: "We endeavour to make the children feel as happy here as possible."[45] The accomplishment of Emmanuel College in pursuing this goal while resisting the imposition of some of the uglier purposes of federal policy was not only that of Revs. Mackay and Taylor but also that of the Indian pupils,[46] parents and leaders who maintained a commitment to education without turning their backs on their cultures and communities.

Notes

1. The mission was located at the foot of what would later become Central Avenue.
2. The fees charged to parents who were Hudson's Bay Company officers or settlers in the region were enough to pay the school teacher's salary.
3. Presumably Indian parents left their children at the mission while they were engaged in hunting activities away from the settlement.
4. The report submitted by Rev. Moore also recommended that "A school for the education of the Indian children and youths should be established and in this school the pupils should be taught to read and write in their own language. . ." (Moore 1873:2). This recommendation was not acted upon, however. Instead, the mission continued to receive a grant from Presbyterian authorities to operate a day school in Prince Albert, to which Indian children were to be admitted without being required to pay fees (Oliver 1934:85). Yet, since the number of Indians visiting Prince Albert decreased significantly during the 1870s, it is not clear that many Indian children were able to take advantage of this arrangement.
5. Within a few months of leaving Prince Albert both Rev. and Mrs. Nisbet died in Manitoba.
6. For further discussion of the Presbyterian School in Prince Albert see Hooper and Fournier 1955 and Dunning 1966.
7. For an account of the optimistic beginnings and unfortunate outcome of the reserve agricultural policy see Dyck 1986. See also Carter 1990.
8. See Newton 1897:82. This amount would have had a value of more than $2.5 million in 1995 dollars.
9. There was also an attempt made to teach the Sioux language at Emmanuel College.
10. See Usher 1971. See also Getty 1974:19–34.
11. SAB B46, 1–2, Address by Bishop McLean, Proceedings of the Synod, Diocese of

Saskatchewan, 4 August 1886, Prince Albert, NWT, pp.10–14.

12. NAC RG10 v.3844 f.73320, 21 October 1890, Petitions from Indians in the Prince Albert area requesting the establishment of an industrial school for Indians in Prince Albert (forwarded to the Superintendent General of Indian Affairs by the Bishop of Saskatchewan and Calgary).

13. Indeed, six of the twelve chiefs who signed Treaty Six at Fort Carlton were Christians.

14. Mackay had spent most of his clerical career as a member of the Church Missionary Society, and the working philosophy of that agency, as outlined above, did not view Aboriginal people as inherently lacking in intelligence or ability.

15. NAC RG10 v.3932 f.117504-1, 23 February 1892, H. Reed, Indian Commissioner, Regina, to L. Vankoughnet, Deputy Superintendent General of Indian Affairs, Ottawa.

16. Canada, Parliament, *Sessional Papers* 1896, Annual Report of the Department of Indian Affairs for 1895, 23 July 1895, J.A. Mackay, Principal of Emmanuel College, to the Superintendent of Indian Affairs, Ottawa, p.51.

17. NAC RG10 v.3844 f.73320, 31 July 1894, H. Reed, Deputy Superintendent of Indian Affairs to T.M. Daly, Superintendent of Indian Affairs.

18. Ibid.

19. At Emmanuel College a half hour was set aside for religious instruction each school day.

20. NAC RG10 v.3932 f.117504-1, 24 June 1895, J.A. Mackay, Principal of Emmanuel College, to the Superintendent of Indian Affairs, Ottawa.

21. SAB A113, V-3 (Mackay Papers in the Innis Papers), 6 November 1897, A.M. Forget, Office of the Indian Commissioner, Winnipeg, to J.A. Mackay, Principal of Emmanuel College.

22. NAC RG10 v.3932 f.117504-1, 11 January 1897, J.A. Mackay, Principal of Emmanuel College, to the Bishop of Saskatchewan and Calgary.

23. Canada, Parliament, *Sessional Papers* 1897, Annual Report of the Department of Indian Affairs for 1896, 2 December 1896, H. Reed, Deputy Superintendent General of Indian Affairs.

24. James Taylor was a graduate of Emmanuel College's discontinued theological training program.

25. Taylor also sought strenuously to have Emmanuel College receive the same per capita grant as the boarding school for Indian children operated by the Roman Catholic Church at Duck Lake.

26. NAC RG10 v.3932 f.117504-1, 20 March 1901, J. Taylor, Principal of Emmanuel College, to D. Laird, Indian Commissioner, Winnipeg.

27. NAC RG10 v.3932 f.117504-1, 13 May 1902, M. Benson, Department of Indian Affairs, Ottawa, to the Secretary, Department of Indian Affairs, Ottawa.

28. For an overview of the "de-tribalization" policy, see Tobias 1986:241–52.

29. By the end of 1900 there were some twenty-nine acres under cultivation at Emmanuel College.

30. In October 1903 forty-two of the forty-nine pupils enrolled at Emmanuel College came from the following reserves: Ahtahkakoop, John Smith, James Smith, James Robert, William Charles, William Twatt and Mistawasis. The remaining seven pupils were identified as "non-treaty." See Canada, Parliament, *Sessional Papers* 1904, Annual Report of the Department of Indian Affairs for 1903, 20 October

1903, J. Taylor, Principal of Emmanuel College, to the Superintendent General of Indian Affairs, pp.363–65.

31. NAC RG10 v.3932 f.117504-1, 8 July 1903, M. Benson, Department of Indian Affairs, Ottawa, to the Deputy Superintendent General, Department of Indian Affairs, Ottawa.

32. NAC RG10 v.3932 f.117504-1, 30 January 1905, J. McKay, Solicitor for Imperial Bank, Prince Albert, to Rev. L.N. Tucker, Secretary, Church of England Missionary Society, Toronto.

33. In his address to the synod, the bishop acknowledged the assistance of a prominent Anglican layman, H.S. Blake, in pressing the case of Emmanuel College to have its debt retired by the government. The bishop also warned that the failure to increase the capitation grant might lead to a reccuring crisis of funding and called for the relationship between church and state in operating such a residential school to be placed in "businesslike terms." See SAB B46, 1–2, Address by Bishop Newnham, Proceedings of Synod, Diocese of Saskatchewan, 24 July 1905, Prince Albert, Saskatchewan.

34. Canada, Parliament, *Sessional Papers* 1903, Annual Report of the Department of Indian Affairs for 1902, 20 August 1902, J. Taylor, Principal of Emmanuel College, to the Superintendent of Indian Affairs, Ottawa, pp.332–34.

35. NAC RG10 v.3932 f.117504-1, 30 April 1903, E.C. Kitchen, Medical Attendant, Prince Albert, to D. Laird, Indian Commissioner, Winnipeg.

36. NAC RG10 v.3932 f.117504-1, 5 July 1904, Dr. J.J. Labrecque, Prince Albert, to Mr. Macarthur, Indian Agent, Duck Lake.

37. Bryce reported that 24 percent of the students and ex-students of boarding and industrial schools had died during the previous fourteen years.

38. NAC RG10 v.4037 f.317021, 1907, P.H. Bryce, Report on the Indian Schools of Manitoba and the North West Territories, Ottawa: Government Printing Bureau.

39. Federal officials calculated that by 1907 some 29 of the 133 children who had attended Emmanuel College had died. They did not, however, choose to emphasize the continuing underfunding of this school by the Department of Indian Affairs as a likely contribution to this high mortality rate.

40. NAC RG10 v.3932 f.117504-1, 30 January 1908, Memorial from the Bishop and Executive Committee of the Diocese of Saskatchewan to the Department of Indian Affairs.

41. NAC RG10 v.3932 f.117504-1, 18 July 1908, W.J. Chisholm, Inspector of Indian Agencies, North Saskatchewan Inspectorate, Prince Albert, to the Indian Commissioner, Winnipeg.

42. The Lac la Ronge Boarding School was built under the supervision of Archdeacon J.A. Mackay who subsequently served as the first principal of this school.

43. NAC RG10 v.3932 f.117504-1, 21 November 1906, M. Benson, Department of Indian Affairs, Ottawa, to Deputy Superintendent General of Indian Affairs, Ottawa.

44. Also all debts incurred by Diocese of Saskatchewan in the operation of Emmanuel College were retired by the federal government upon the closure of the institution. See NAC RG10 v.3932 f.117504-1, 8 July 1907, Internal Department of Indian Affairs Memorandum to the Deputy Superintendent General of Indian Affairs, Ottawa.

45. Canada, Parliament, *Sessional Papers* 1903, Annual Report of the Department of

Indian Affairs for 1902, 20 August 1902, J. Taylor, Principal of Emmanuel College, to the Superintendent of Indian Affairs, Ottawa, pp.332–34.

46. Included among these pupils were Edward Ahenakew who became a canon in the Anglican Church and who also served during the early 1920s as the president in Western Canada of the League of Indians of Canada, the first national Indian political organization. By the early 1920s Ahenakew had become sharply critical of the defects of residential schooling for Indians. See Ahenakew 1973:130–35.

Chapter 3

The Return to Prince Albert

St. Alban's and All Saints Residential Schools

In the years between the closure of Emmanuel College and the resumption of residential schooling for Indians in Prince Albert in 1944 Canadian society experienced the impact of two world wars and the Great Depression. The administration of the Department of Indian Affairs, however, remained largely unchanged during this period. Notwithstanding its transformation into the Indian Affairs Branch (within the Department of Mines and Resources) during the 1930s, the department's traditional policies and procedures became steadily more entrenched at a time when much of the rest of the country was undergoing fundamental revision. Although the enactment of federal legislation in 1920 did make schooling compulsory for Indian children, with the onset of the Depression and the declaration of the Second World War there was a chronic shortage of funding to provide adequate facilities and programming for Indian pupils.

The Diocese of Saskatchewan's involvement in residential schooling did not end with the closure of Emmanuel College. It continued to conduct federally-funded residential schools at Lac la Ronge and Onion Lake as well as the Battleford Industrial School, which remained in operation until 1914. Within Prince Albert the St. Alban's Ladies College enjoyed the use of its new building (which officially opened in 1908) located across the street from the Prince Albert Collegiate Institute (PACI). Although St. Alban's had been intended to serve as a fee-paying high school for girls, it was unable to attract sufficient revenue to survive. When the Ladies College was phased out in the late 1920s, the building was re-opened as St. George's Boys Residence and provided accommodation for students from outside Prince Albert who attended high school at PACI. The vast majority of the boys who stayed at St. George's were non-Indians, but a few Indian students stayed at the residence and attended classes at PACI during the early 1930s.[1] The department paid grants to St. George's on behalf of these Indian high school students, an arrangement that was staunchly endorsed by Archdeacon Paul of the Diocese of Saskatchewan:

this plan of bringing suitable Indian boys to study at white High

Schools has proved successful. It gives them the confidence of mixing with white people, makes them fluent in speaking English, and fits them to take their place as citizens of our country.

But . . . in order to make full use of this plan, and raise Indian homes and Indian life to a higher level, the educated Indian men must have educated wives, and some of the progressive Indian men have been handicapped, because their wives have not had the same opportunities of education that they have had themselves.[2]

Paul suggested that some of the more able Indian grade eight female pupils should be sent to Saskatoon where they might reside in the teacher's hostel and attend local high schools.

Shortly before the closure of St. George's at the end of the 1930s, the Synod of the Diocese of Saskatchewan passed a resolution calling for the facility to be offered to the federal government for use as a residential school for higher education and vocational training for Indian pupils.[3] Although in their official response federal officials cited economic circumstances as making it unlikely that any new residential schools would be created in the foreseeable future,[4] an internal departmental memorandum written by the Inspector of Indian Agencies for Saskatchewan expressed serious doubts concerning the purposes and quality of the work being done in residential schools:

> I am not at all opposed to religious instruction, in fact I am strongly in favour of it and consider it absolutely necessary, but it makes my blood boil to go out on our Reserves and find I can do so little to rectify conditions, owing to lack of funds, and at the same time see thousands of dollars spent by our Department under the guise of educating the Indians when it is actually being spent on teaching denominational religion. The churches pride themselves on what they have done for the Indians, and shout it from the housetops. They advocate higher education, and ask the Department to pay for it. They want the spending of the money, but when it comes to placing those Indians, after they have received the higher education, they look to the Department to do it. In their work in the residential schools, they have to a large extent forgotten what Christianity means. They are simply seeking ways and means of taking every opportunity of getting our Department to pay the expenses of their missionaries, in order that they may increase the number of their particular denomination. If they were honest with the people, a great many of them would openly acknowledge that it is not Christianity, but denominationalism, they are teaching, and would substitute the word "church" for "God."[5]

In any case, the war effort soon took precedence over the erection of new residential schools for Indian children in spite of efforts by the Anglican Church to acquire a federally-funded Indian school to relieve it of the costs of maintaining and paying municipal taxes on the St. Alban's facility.[6]

From Onion Lake to St. Alban's

The situation changed suddenly in December 1943 when the Anglican residential school at Onion Lake was destroyed by fire. At the time of the accident the school had an authorized pupilage of 100 and actual attendance of some 116 children.[7] Within days the Bishop of Saskatchewan was in touch with Ottawa, stressing the need to continue the children's education and offering the use of the St. Alban's building as a replacement facility. The bishop advised that only minor renovations would be required to prepare the building for use.

The relocation of the Onion Lake School to the St. Alban's facility[8] in Prince Albert was agreed upon quickly by officials of the Indian Affairs Branch and the Anglican Church. The pupilage of the school would remain at one hundred, and the branch agreed to spend some $2,000 per annum to repair and maintain the building in lieu of rent. This arrangement was expected to last at least five years. Beds for the new school were to be supplied by the Department of National Defence, while the Kingston Penitentiary was asked to supply 300 of the new felt blankets manufactured at that institution.[9] Concern was expressed by the minister in charge of the Indian Affairs Branch regarding the lack of readily available land near St. Alban's for the purpose of continuing the vocational agricultural training that had been such a central feature of the school curriculum at Onion Lake,[10] and he indicated his hope that steps might be taken to rectify this deficiency. The principal of the Onion Lake Indian Residential School, Rev. H. Ellis, moved to Prince Albert to oversee the renovations and make preparations to resume classes at the relocated institution. By April 1944 all of the staff and fifty of the students had been moved to St. Alban's. It had taken three months to rectify a number of unforeseen problems, including the replacement of frozen water pipes and extensive repairs to the heating plant. Branch officials were dismayed by the greater than anticipated cost of putting the building right[11] but, under the circumstances, had no alternative but to proceed with the work. Moreover, given the relatively substantial costs invested into relocating the school to St. Alban's, there was scant interest within government for requests to rebuild the school at its original location near Onion Lake,[12] even though the Missionary Service of the Church of England in Canada[13] (MSCC) continued the operation of the school farm at Onion Lake for some time in the hope that this might happen.[14]

The opening of St. Alban's sparked an increase in the number of children for whom admission to residential school was sought. In December 1944 there were 150 children in a school that, according to branch calculations, had a capacity for a maximum of 122 pupils in its dormitories and an official pupilage of 125. Church authorities explained that pressure to admit more children to St. Alban's than could readily be accommodated was fueled not by a denominational desire to recruit additional adherents but by IAB field staff and Indian parents.[15] The Anglicans further suggested that some of the children from Montreal Lake then attending St. Alban's might be sent north to the Lac la Ronge Indian Residential School where there were fewer pupils enrolled than the allowed pupilage of 100.

Throughout its existence St. Alban's Indian Residential School suffered from overcrowding, a circumstance that was interpreted variously by different officials. A school inspector employed by the Indian Affairs Branch visited the school just prior to Christmas 1945 and observed teachers working with their classes. The grade one class, which had thirty-four pupils present that day out of a class of thirty-nine, was judged to exhibit very good "pupil conduct habits":

> The attitude to school life appears to be wholesome. Work habits were very steady and workmanship especially good. Class response is ready and thoughtful. I believe the quality and efficiency of the learning process in this room is very good indeed.
>
> As indicated above [the teacher's] . . . technique of teaching compares favorably with that of our best primary teachers in public schools.[16]

About a joint grade one and two class of thirty-one pupils, the Inspector observed that:

> Conduct habits are good. The pupils' attitude to school life also appears to be good. Seat industry was fairly good and workmanship good. Class response is fairly ready and thoughtful. The general learning plane is wholesome. The room is in safe hands.[17]

A rather different assessment was submitted by the regional Inspector of Indian Agencies, Mr. Ostrander, after an inspection of the school's facilities some four months later. St. Alban's was, in his view, suffering seriously from being "very definitely overcrowded":

> Nineteen senior girls sleep in single beds . . .; 53 intermediate girls sleep in . . . 38 cots. Fifteen of these cots have two girls sleeping in each one. Thirty-nine junior boys sleep in . . . [23] cots, and [16] of these cots have two boys sleeping in them. Twenty-two senior boys are sleeping . . . with one boy in each bed. Two of the classrooms are very decidedly overcrowded with not sufficient seats for the pupils and no room for the necessary desks if they had them.[18]

Ostrander suggested that insufficient thought had been given to the health of the children in permitting such sleeping arrangements and recommended that the number of children in the residence be reduced to one hundred at the beginning of the next term. He also noted a serious lack of playground space for the children. While permission had been granted to St. Alban's to use the PACI playgrounds whenever these were available, boys at St. Alban's told the inspector that they had been allowed to play on these grounds only three times during the previous month. The inspector concluded that the high rate of absconding (also identified as "truancy" or "runaways") at St. Alban's resulted at least in part from its lack of recreational facilities and inadequate supervision of the pupils. Indeed, Ostrander mentioned that when he had visited James Smith Reserve a week after inspecting St. Alban's, two boys from that band attending the residential school in Prince Albert had simply walked all the way home, crossing the river near Fenton on a railway bridge that was dangerous for use by pedestrians. Although Ostrander allowed that Rev. Ellis, the principal, was a "good manager trying to make the best of a bad situation" and that some education was being imparted in spite of the poor classroom facilities, he stated that the cramped conditions in St. Alban's made it a fire hazard that should not be permitted to continue as it was:

> More than one disastrous Indian school fire has been started by the pupils themselves in an effort to obtain their freedom from a school which they did not like. The number of truants in this school would certainly indicate much dissatisfaction, and there are hundreds of places in the building where irresponsible Indian boys might start a fire very easily.
>
> I realize that the Anglican Church was permitted to re-open the St. Alban's School in their building at Prince Albert after the Onion Lake fire and that the need was urgent and more or less a temporary war measure. However, I do not think that this school should be permitted to continue very much longer in a very unsuitable building amongst unsuitable surroundings. Certainly the enrolment should be considerably reduced and I would say that the dissatisfied boys, who are, in my opinion, a menace to the lives of the other children, should be the ones discharged and as soon as possible.[19]

The Secretary of the Indian and Eskimo Residential School Commission of the MSCC conceded Ostrander's criticisms of the St. Alban's facility, but claimed that overenrolment in the school was due primarily to orphans and other needy Indian children being sent to the school by IAB field personnel without prior authorization.[20] For instance, two daughters of an Indian woman who was admitted to the Prince Albert Sanitarium were simply dispatched to St. Alban's; the school principal had been unwilling to turn them away. The Bishop of Saskatchewan subsequently expressed his disagreement with Ostrander's view that St. Alban's was a fire hazard, yet promised that he would do all in his power to remove "as far as is humanly possible every danger of fire."[21] Clearly, the Diocese of Saskatchewan was determined to maintain an Indian residential school at St. Alban's.[22] This objective was supported by mounting evidence of a much greater need for residential schooling capacity within the district than even the oversubscribed St. Alban's Indian Residential School could hope to satisfy on its own.

The Loss of the Lac la Ronge Indian Residential School

The situation deteriorated further in February 1947 when the Lac la Ronge Indian Residential School was levelled by fire.[23] Within days most of the pupils had been returned to their homes by airplane or car and a few others transferred to Gordon's Indian Residential School in southern Saskatchewan. Aside from St. Alban's, Gordon's was the only remaining Anglican residential institution in the province.

A police investigation determined that the school fire at Lac la Ronge had been intentionally set by a twelve-year-old boy who had been given the matches to do so by a fifteen-year-old boy. Since the boys had readily admitted their guilt, officials of the Indian Affairs Branch initially saw little point in taking further action against them. The Inspector of Indian Agencies in Saskatchewan advised the RCMP that, while he believed in the use of punishment where it might do some good, he thought that if the two boys who had admitting setting the fire were sentenced to the provincial reformatory they would "learn more about crime and misdemeanour . . . than they have learned, or will learn, in their home environment."[24] Nonetheless, the former principal at Lac la Ronge, Rev. Wickenden, insisted that punitive action had to be taken:

> Failure to bring them to trial in a court of law will only be interpreted as a sign of weak indulgence and indifference. There will be for these young delinquents and their associates no such thing as the "majesty of the law", but rather a growing disregard for all law and order and a corresponding contempt for officers of the law. I cannot conceive that offences of a similar nature would be overlooked in civilized society, and it is our task to Christianize our Indian wards and to instill into them a healthy respect for the white man's justice.[25]

In the end, IAB officials in Ottawa were shamed into action by the Rev. Wickenden's argument and opted to prosecute the younger boy who had lit the fire. The boy was in due course sentenced to the provincial reformatory in Regina. Almost two years after the school fire the Director of Corrections for Saskatchewan contacted regional IAB officials to ask where and to whom the boy, now aged fourteen years, might be released. He was the best student in his grade at the reformatory,[26] and corrections officials—who saw little point in him spending any further time in custody—were keen to speed up arrangements for his release. Their approach to dealing with the boy contrasted sharply with that of the Rev. Wickenden, who was employed and empowered to oversee the moral, social and educational development of Indian children.

The question of whether the Lac la Ronge Indian Residential School ought to be rebuilt or relocated engendered a spirited debate between the Anglican Church and the Indian Affairs Branch. The Bishop of Saskatchewan was determined to do all that he could to persuade the federal government to rebuild both the Onion Lake and Lac la Ronge residential schools, thereby maintaining the proportion of Anglican institutions in Saskatchewan engaged in "Indian work" to those operated by the Anglicans' chief competitors, the Roman Catholics. Regional IAB officials, on the other hand, argued in favour of replacing the Onion Lake and Lac la Ronge schools with one new residential school that might also permit the closure of St. Alban's. The establishment of a single, large residential school on the Little Red River Reserve, north of Prince Albert, would permit the establishment of a full agricultural operation in conjunction with the school. The bishop countered with the observation that such agricultural training would be a waste of time for Indian children from the north who would, upon graduation, be returning to decidedly non-agricultural ways of life in the north. IAB officials, however, saw no particular reason why all Indian children should not eat well at residential school, wherever they might live after their school years.[27] The underlying assumption was that Indian children would continue to play a central part in growing much of the food used to prepare their meals, as had been the tradition at many residential schools in Western Canada.[28]

The Director of the Indian School Administration of the Anglican Church's MSCC formulated a compromise proposal that called for: (1) the construction of day schools at Onion Lake, Lac la Ronge, Stanley Mission and other suitable points; (2) construction of a new Anglican residential school for at least 150 pupils somewhere north of Prince Albert; and (3) continued use of St. Alban's as a hostel or centre of higher education for advanced students from various Indian schools.[29] By this time, however, federal officials had begun to consider another option to ease the substantial backlog of Indian residential schools that had been destroyed by fire or otherwise allowed to run down during the Depression and war years across the country. On the same day that the Secretary of the Indian School Administration wrote to communicate the Anglican Church's compromise proposal to the Indian Affairs Branch, the IAB Superintendent of Welfare and Training contacted the federal government's Crown Assets Allocation Committee to ask whether a surplus military training camp[30] located on the southwest side of Prince Albert might be available for use as a residential school facility.[31]

While preliminary planning proceeded for a new Anglican residential school somewhere in the vicinity of Prince Albert, St. Alban's continued to labour under a much larger enrolment than it was designed to handle. A new principal, the Rev. G.W. Fisher,[32] encountered the same problems as his predecessor,[33] yet doggedly strove to maintain operations at St. Alban's through a series of makeshift arrangements. The bed linen for the dormitories at St. Alban's was donated by the Ottawa Branch of the Anglican Church's Women's Auxiliary, while the local penitentiary provided some vegetables to reduce expenditures within the school.[34] Due to a lack of manual training facilities at the school, some of the boys had been permitted to do odd jobs for residents of Prince Albert, an arrangement that was viewed as being "beneficial to behaviour and profitable for the boys."[35] Only three girls and two boys staying at St. Alban's were enrolled in high school classes at PACI, and an IAB official reported that all of the teachers appeared "to be doing good work and getting at least average (for Indians) results."[36] However well-meaning church and government officials may have been in pursuing their duties, the provision of residential schooling in Prince Albert for Indian children was evidently viewed more as a voluntary, charitable endeavour than as a treaty obligation that warranted appropriate levels of funding.

Moving to the Army Barracks

By the end of 1947 an IAB proposal to take possession of the former Canadian Army training base in Prince Albert and to establish an Indian residential school there under the auspices of the Anglican Church had been accepted by the Indian Schools Administration of the MSCC.[37] Although the new school was not scheduled to open until September 1948, overcrowding at St. Alban's prompted Rev. Fisher to recommend that the boys enrolled at St. Alban's might be housed at the military camp for the remainder of the 1947–48 school year while continuing to return to St. Alban's by truck for their meals and classes each day.[38] By the end of that school year, some fifty boys were making the daily trip to and from St. Alban's. Nonetheless, lack of sufficient instructional space at St. Alban's resulted in most pupils attending classes on a half-day basis.[39] Due to bureaucratic difficulties encountered in calculating an appropriate level of federal funding for the school, St. Alban's remained so short-staffed that the Rev. Fisher felt obliged to return to work almost immediately after being discharged from hospital, despite his weakened condition due to illness and his advanced years.[40]

Government and church officials anticipated that opening All Saints Indian Residential School[41] at the former military base would rectify the logistical difficulties experienced both at St. Alban's and the MSCC-operated Elkhorn Residential School in Manitoba. The military base featured a substantial number of roughly-finished and partially-serviced barrack huts along with a drill hall and kitchen, laundry and medical facilities. Initial plans in May 1948 allowed the new All Saints School to have a pupilage of between 120 and 180 children, while the Elkhorn Institution would experience an offsetting reduction in its pupilage by 70.[42] The lease on St. Alban's would be renewed on a short-term basis until the future of this institution could be determined. Nonetheless, IAB officials viewed the new All Saints facility as having the potential to house up to 400 pupils and, thus, took steps to secure control over the entire facility lest the provincial government request the use of additional buildings from the Department of Public Works.[43] By the end of June 1948 the scope of the as yet unopened All Saints School was substantially increased with the decision to close the Elkhorn School. Accordingly, All Saints would be required to serve 400 pupils by January 1949 and a further 200 pupils the following September.[44] In a matter of months the number of Indian children attending residential schools in Prince Albert would almost triple. While much attention was devoted to ensuring adequate accommodation at the new school, detailed consideration of the levels of staffing and funding required to provide suitable child care and educational programs at both All Saints and St. Alban's seemed to have been largely overlooked.

When the new school year began in the fall of 1948 Rev. Fisher, who served as principal of both All Saints and St. Alban's, was instructed to keep duplication of services between the two schools to a minimum.[45] St. Alban's was to provide accommodation for girls attending high school at PACI and other elementary school-aged girls. Co-educational classes would be held for children from grades four to eight, thus requiring girls in these grades housed at St. Alban's to walk to and from All Saints daily:

> The walking involved in the passage of the girls from one school to the other should provide an opportunity to improve the lackadaisical posture and gait of pupils in whom these defects are not chargeable to dietary deficiency.[46]

There was also an expectation of assistance to be rendered by the older pupils, particularly the girls:

> ... there are likely to be many bigger girls who, although they have done little book work, are intelligent and capable of being trained quickly to be useful around the school.[47]

Given the dispersed pattern of the huts at the new campus, the election of pupil group leaders was recommended to assist in governing the student body, although the selection of class leaders or, more accurately, monitors would have to pass the scrutiny of the school authorities. Finally, IAB officials expected that vocational training in agriculture, cattle-raising, gardening and sewing would in due course become integral features of the curriculum.

Whatever the hopes had been for the new arrangement, the fall term of 1948 proved to be an organizational disaster. The local Indian agent reported in September that the school was progressing "very unsatisfactorily":

Two-thirds of the staff are old and decrepit. Organized games and sports have been lacking, which has resulted in a steady stream of children, boys and girls, running away. Further, indifferent supervision has permitted pupils to wander downtown, complaints of petty thievery have been received.[48]

The principal rapidly fell behind in his paperwork as he sought to respond to these and other problems. Late in October he explained to his superiors in the Indian Schools Administration of the MSCC that since the beginning of the school term he had travelled more than 1,600 miles trying to get children to return to school:

> I am really in despair. Many of these runaways have been off four and five times. It is hard to know just what to do. I really feel like turning some of them out of the school altogether, but this is probably what many of them would like me to do, and others might do the same in order to get out also.[49]

Word of poor conditions at the new school spread throughout the district, and some children were simply taken home by parents who were disturbed by complaints about the inadequacies of food, clothing and cleanliness provided to pupils at All Saints.[50] A number of parents, chiefs, councillors and other Indian leaders (including John Tootoosis[51]) came to the school to investigate conditions, a development that was not popular with IAB officials:

> This could become a nuisance. Indians should be restricted to visiting their children in a place appointed therefore, and anyone other than a departmental official who wants to do any investigating should first have the permission of the [Agency] Superintendent.[52]

From the perspective of IAB officials, the appropriate division of labour between themselves and Anglican staff personnel was not being observed by the latter:

> There is either a failure to understand or refusal to admit that it is the function of departmental officials to designate where and when an Indian child is to attend school. "Recruiting" has proceeded as if schools were still at the church-owned mission stage of development when parents were induced rather than required to put their children in school. Recruiting and pursuing children has caused the Principal to be absent from school at a time when it would have been better to be preparing to receive the children into a place adequately equipped, supplied, and organized to make conditions as attractive as possible. . . .[53]

As if things were not bad enough, an epidemic of mumps[54] struck many children and staff members, thus further retarding activities at the schools. The discovery by IAB officials that three young boys were still housed at St. Alban's and sleeping in the girls' dormitory triggered a demand to the principal that the youngsters be transferred to All Saints immediately: "Admittedly they are small boys, but the behaviour-patterns of primitive people in respect to sex are unfortunately too predictable to make this arrangement a wise one."[55] An Indian man who had been hired by the MSCC as a boys' supervisor at All Saints explained to the Inspector of Indian Agencies for Saskatchewan that the school appeared to have "no organization whatsoever. Nobody seems to have any authority to say yes or no to anything."[56] Similar reports were made by other IAB staff who visited the school. The question of whether pupils should be permitted to return to their homes during the Christmas vacation was dealt with by the principal not in terms of the children's desire to see their parents or requests made by many parents to have their children home for the holidays but with respect to the possible costs that this course of action might entail. The principal preferred not to allow the children to leave the school lest they might leave some of their school-issued clothing at home and need to be given new outfits on their return to Prince Albert, thus adding to the cost of operating the schools.[57]

Relations between church and IAB officials worsened when the Secretary of the Indian Schools Administration of the MSCC charged the federal government with providing inappropriate facilities for residential schooling in Prince Albert and elsewhere in Western Canada. IAB officials countered with complaints about the poor quality of staff members provided to All Saints and St. Alban's by the MSCC. In way of protesting conditions at All Saints, certain members of the school staff insisted upon wearing their overcoats and overshoes indoors, even though their pupils were dressed in shirt sleeves and light dresses.[58] Due to the shortage of staff, teachers at St. Alban's were asked to assist with supervising students in the dormitories, and school staff members at All Saints were expected by IAB officials to assist in repairing broken windows. The refusal by school staff to take on additional duties and the rumour that some of them might resign unless the federal government took action to improve the situation prompted the regional Inspector of Indian Agencies to suggest that any such resignations would not comprise much of a loss to the overall operation of the schools.[59]

To round off a chaotic fall term at the schools, the provincial fire inspector called for immediate measures to be taken at St. Alban's to install a fire door on the boiler room, new doors for the fire escapes, a fire alarm system for the top floor and self-closing doors onto all stairways in the building.[60] Rev. Fisher, who was so occupied with other emergencies at the schools that he did not find the time even to seek estimates on the cost of providing the required renovations, was, in the end, unable to supervise the repairs. He died shortly before classes recommenced in the New Year.

Emerging from Chaos

Mr. Mayo, who had previously served at Gordon's Indian Residential School, took over as acting principal of All Saints while the matron at St. Alban's, Miss Jones, oversaw operations there. One woman, an eleven-year-old All Saints student during this period, remembers it as a very bad time:

> This was not a happy school. I was shocked by all the fighting and bullying that went on. I learned to keep my mouth shut when I knew who did things they were not supposed to do. But it didn't help. Usually the whole dormitory was punished until they found out who was guilty. Some of the staff were pretty mean too and did things that were not right—such as pulling ears, slapping heads, and hitting knuckles.
>
> I remember being hungry most of the time, as the meals were not very good. We had supper so early and we would really be hungry by breakfast time.
>
> . . . The one thing I will never forget was when I told the principal that I could not speak Cree.
>
> It happened like this. My older brother . . . had run away from school and had gone back to the reserve. I got called to the office. There, the principal told me that I was heard saying in Cree that I was going to run away too if my brother hadn't come back.
>
> I told him, "I'm sorry Mr. Mayo but I couldn't say that in Cree because I don't talk Cree."
>
> He said "Don't be stupid, all Indians speak Cree." Then he jumped up, grabbed his strap and hit me all over the back, arms and legs and head. It was the worst strapping of my whole life. I didn't understand it. I saw other students strapped for speaking Cree, now I was being strapped for not speaking it.
>
> He thought I was lying but . . . what I said was true. . . . Thank goodness, Mr. Mayo was only a substitute principal and we only had to put up with him for a few months. (Bear 1991:43–44)

Before the end of the school year Rev. A.J. Scrase was appointed the new principal at All Saints[61] and a separate principal, Rev. N.D. Pilcher, was hired for St. Alban's. The death of Rev. Fisher apparently persuaded both MSCC and IAB officials that the job of running both schools was too much for one person to manage. Nonetheless, at the end of an extraordinarily unsettling year of residential schooling operations in Prince Albert, Rev. Scrase found himself having to battle with IAB officials over the cost of repairing the school's large, open-boxed truck so that it could be used to transport pupils to their home reserves.

This final episode seemed to symbolize the confusion and displacement of priorities that surrounded church and government operations with respect to All

Saints and St. Alban's throughout the 1948–49 year. The principal and the local Indian agent disagreed about whether the estimated $290 required to make the truck roadworthy ought to be paid from the school's budget (which was funded by the federal government) or directly by IAB. The fact that Indian children were to be transported over considerable distances to their home reserves in an open-boxed truck, exposed to the elements, road dust and exhaust fumes discharged from a short tail-pipe that ended just behind the cab of the truck[62] was accepted without comment while the representatives of church and state haggled over which side would pick up what amounted to an essential but scarcely sufficient expenditure.[63]

The situation in the two schools did, however, improve during the 1949–50 school year. Local IAB officials reported that the relationship between pupils and staff "has greatly improved at the All Saints Residential School. The whole set-up has a totally different atmosphere. St. Alban's too is operating quite smoothly."[64] The temporary closure of Gordon's Indian Residential School, due to its water supply receding beyond the danger level, resulted in twenty-nine of its pupils being transferred to All Saints, raising the total enrolment there to 253, although IAB officials noted that it could be readily fitted to accommodate more than this number.[65] A hockey team from All Saints competed in the city league, winning the championship under their coach, Rev. Scrase.[66]

While St. Alban's was, in the opinion of IAB personnel, now "well able to endure inspection by visitors,"[67] it was not viewed as being "frozen" in its current pattern. It was suggested that in due course the younger girls be transferred to All Saints leaving St. Alban's for use by older girls in the higher grades. In the meantime, great reliance had been placed upon over-age girls to give "leadership in housekeeping and other activities." The use of pupils' labour in operating the schools had prompted the new principal to wonder whether St. Alban's might not be viewed as slipping into a "half-day" system with respect to the schooling of at least some of its older girls. Accordingly, Rev. Pilcher employed additional laundry workers to permit the older girls to pursue their studies on a full-time basis. IAB personnel sought to allay his fears about the practice of using pupils to reduce the need for paid laundry assistants:

> I assured [Rev. Pilcher] he would not be accused of continuing the half-day system so long as there were desks for all pupils and so long as a reasonable amount of practical work in laundering, cooking, mending, etc., is required of pupils so that they become competent in the theory and practice of these household science subjects. Unfortunately, some of his staff do not appreciate the necessity or the method of integrating this work with the pupils' schooling in the classroom. We must assume that advice on this subject must be repeated year after year and the organization of schools must be examined periodically to check any retrogression.

.... The part-time service of enough older girls can be assured as long as there is a quota of the academically-retarded.[68]

The principal acknowledged these instructions, indicating his agreement with how necessary "practical and adequate training in domestic science is for our girls."[69]

At the beginning of the 1950–51 school year there were 314 pupils enrolled at All Saints with more still to arrive from the Red Earth Indian Day School. It was, however, difficult to obtain a sufficient number of girls in grades one to four to occupy all one hundred spaces at St. Alban's, particularly since a number of families specifically requested that all of their children be together at one school.[70] Disciplinary problems were also emerging as a concern at St. Alban's. Two of the fourteen-year-old girls at the school ran away from the school repeatedly, in spite of having been strapped "within the instructions given by officers of the Department."[71] Of particular concern to Rev. Pilcher was the likelihood that the girls might be taken as being sixteen years of age or even older; in his view, the matter was "much more serious for all concerned now that these girls have reached maturity."[72] The solution he proposed was to remove the girls from the school if they continued to run away for, in the principal's view, "the school cannot be a prison."[73] Indeed, only by breaking the fire regulations and locking the girls in their rooms could they be prevented from escaping. Misgivings about the quality of dormitory supervision at All Saints were also expressed by senior IAB officials from Ottawa after they inspected the school:

> I was not at all impressed with the supervision at this school. .... There seems to be no control or discipline in the dormitories and the condition thereof is not a credit to the Principal and his staff. The Reverend Scrase places the blame entirely on the poor calibre of the supervisors supplied to him by the ISA. On the other hand, his teaching staff is quite good as the inspection reports hereunder would indicate.[74]

Increasingly surliness and inattentive classroom behaviour on the part of the older children at St. Alban's coincided with growing uneasiness among MSCC and IAB officials concerning the physical limitations of the St. Alban's facility[75] and the logistical demands of operating two residential schools at separate locations in one city.[76] The high costs of running a now forty-year-old facility that had limited recreational facilities, poor staff accommodation and a persistently high fire-hazard rating inclined church and federal government officials to agree about the advantages of moving the remaining grade one to four girls from St. Alban's to All Saints. But if this course of action was to be adopted, the Diocese of Saskatchewan requested that two separate schools ought to be maintained on the same site: all boys would attend All Saints and all girls would attend St. Alban's.[77] Apparently the diocese was less concerned with the principle of gender segregation than it was with maintaining the existence of two distinct Anglican residential schools, one of which might one day be returned to Onion Lake.

In the end the decision to amalgamate St. Alban's with All Saints refuted the fiction that there were two Indian residential schools temporarily located in Prince Albert, one or both of which might someday be returned to their previous locations. Henceforth there was to be one government-owned but Anglican-operated Indian residential school in the city and in the Diocese of Saskatchewan, and there was little chance that it would be removed from Prince Albert in the foreseeable future.

For a time it was proposed that the now abandoned, church-owned St. Alban's facility might temporarily be leased to the United Church as a home for one of its residential schools, although MSCC officials preferred a plan that would transform St. Alban's into a hostel for high school students who attended PACI.[78] In the end neither possibility came to pass. The building was sold by the Diocese of Saskatchewan to the Roman Catholic Church, which operated a boys' school there before moving it south of Prince Albert to the town of St. Louis. The building was eventually demolished to make way for an apartment building.

Notes

1. ADSA, Box 53, Indian Work Reports 1934–42, 25 April 1934, Archdeacon W.E.J. Paul, Prince Albert, to the Secretary, Department of Indian Affairs, Ottawa.
2. Ibid.
3. ADSA, Box 53, Indian Affairs Day Schools, etc. file, 23 June 1938, Bishop Hurd, Prince Albert, to R.A. Hoey, Superintendent of Welfare and Training, IAB, Ottawa. Bishop Hurd claimed that the building had been erected at a cost of $80,000 and was capable of housing fifty children. The diocese was, according to Hurd, willing to hand over the building to the IAB at no cost provided that the facility would be used for "the educational work of Indians in the Diocese."
4. ADSA, Box 53, Indian Affairs Day Schools, etc. file, 16 November 1938, R.A. Hoey, Superintendent of Welfare and Training, IAB, Ottawa, to Bishop Hurd, Prince Albert.
5. NAC RG10 v.8754 f.651/25-1 pt.1, 26 January 1939, T. Robertson, Inspector of Indian Agencies, IAB, Regina, to R.A. Hoey, Superintendent of Welfare and Training, Indian Affairs Branch, Ottawa.
6. The Diocese of Saskatchewan was required to pay annual local property taxes on the building by the City of Prince Albert. The tax rate would be considerably reduced if the building was used for educational purposes. See NAC RG10 v.6320 f.658-1 pt.2, 13 December 1943, Dr. H.A. Alderwood, Secretary, Indian and Eskimo Residential School Commission, Missionary Society of the Church in Canada, Winnipeg, to T.A. Crerar, Minister of Mines and Resources. Indeed, by the end of 1943 the Diocese of Saskatchewan had outstanding tax arrears on the building amounting to more than $2,000; see NAC RG10 v.6320 f.658-1 pt.2, 14 December 1943, Newspaper clipping from the Prince Albert *Daily Herald*, entitled

"St. George's to accommodate 80 pupils as Indian school."

7. The children at the school came from five different agencies: Battleford (thirty-nine), Onion Lake (nineteen), Carlton (forty-eight), Saddle Lake (seven), and Duck Lake (three). See NAC RG10 v.6320 f.658-1 pt.2, 13 December 1943, M. Christianson, General Superintendent of Indian Agencies, IAB, Regina, to the Indian Affairs Branch, Ottawa.

8. Until its closure in 1951 this relocated school continued to be identified in correspondence by some employees of the Indian Affairs Branch (particularly those in Ottawa) as the "Onion Lake Church of England Indian Residential School in Prince Albert." Locally it tended to be identified as "St. Alban's Indian Residential School." Members of the Diocese of Saskatchewan and the representatives of the Indian and Eskimo Residential School Commission, Missionary Society of the Church in Canada, also came to identify it as "St. Alban's."

9. NAC RG10 v.6322 f.658-5 pt.9, 8 January 1944, Warden, Kingston Penitentiary, to Indian Affairs Branch, Ottawa.

10. NAC RG10 v.6320 f.658-1 pt.2, 8 December 1943, T.A. Crerar, Minister of Mines and Resources, to Dr. H.A. Alderwood, Secretary, Indian and Eskimo Residential School Commission, Missionary Society of the Church in Canada, Winnipeg.

11. In the end, the overall costs of repairing the building and acquiring new equipment for the school cost over $14,000. See NAC RG10 v.6320 f.658-1 pt.2, 19 April 1944, R.A. Hoey, Superintendent of Welfare and Training, IAB, Ottawa, to Dr. H.A. Alderwood, Secretary, Indian and Eskimo Residential School Commission, Missionary Society of the Church in Canada, Winnipeg.

12. NAC RG10 v.6322 f.658-5 pt.9, 15 May 1944, M. Christianson, General Superintendent of Indian Agencies, Indian Affairs Branch, Regina, to Indian Affairs Branch, Ottawa.

13. This was the Anglican Church agency that oversaw the operations of Anglican Indian and Eskimo residential schools across Canada. It dealt directly with the headquarters of the Indian Affairs Branch in Ottawa not only on policy matters but also concerning administrative difficulties involving particular schools. Anglican residential school personnel were employees of the ISA of the MSCC.

14. NAC RG10 v.6322 f.658-5 pt.9, 24 October 1944, Dr. H.A. Alderwood, Secretary, Indian and Eskimo Residential School Commission, Missionary Society of the Church in Canada, Winnipeg, to Dr. H.W. McGill, IAB, Ottawa.

15. NAC RG10 v.6320 f.658-1 pt.2, 15 December 1944, Dr. H.A. Alderwood, Secretary, Indian and Eskimo Residential School Commission, Missionary Society of the Church in Canada, Ottawa, to R.A. Hoey, Acting Director, IAB, Ottawa.

16. NAC RG10 v.6323 f.658-6 pt.1, 20 December 1945, Inspector's Report on St. Alban's Indian Residential School.

17. Ibid.

18. NAC RG10 v.6320 f.658-1 pt.2, 30 April 1946, J.P.B. Ostrander, Inspector of Indian Agencies, IAB, Regina, to IAB, Ottawa.

19. Ibid.

20. NAC RG10 v.6320 f.658-1 pt.2, 17 May 1946, Dr. H.A. Alderwood, Secretary, Indian and Eskimo Residential School Commission, Missionary Society of the Church in Canada, Ottawa, to P. Phelan, IAB, Ottawa.

21. NAC RG10 v.6320 f.658-1 pt.2, 23 May 1946, Bishop of Saskatchewan, Prince Albert, to R.A. Hoey, Director, IAB, Ottawa.

22. This determination continued despite sustained haggling among the Diocese of Saskatchewan, the Indian and Eskimo Residential School Commission of the MSCC and the federal government, concerning the respective financial responsibilities of each of these three parties for maintaining the building within which St. Alban's was housed. See ADSA, Box 53, Residential Schools File, 1933-59, 8 March 1946, Bishop H.D. Martin, Prince Albert, to Rev. H.A. Alderwood, IERSC, MSCC, Winnipeg for a particularly fraught example of this discourse: Bishop Martin wrote, ". . . I do admit making many mistakes among which apparently is the fact that I offered you the use of St. Alban's when the Onion Lake building burnt down."

23. NAC RG10 v.8754 f.651/25-1 pt.1, 4 February 1947, Memorandum from the Director, Indian Affairs Branch, Ottawa, to the Deputy Minister of Mines and Resources.

24. NAC RG10 v.8754 f.651/25-1 pt.1, 31 May 1947, J.P.B. Ostrander, Inspector of Indian Agencies, IAB, Regina, to W. Mortimer, Superintendent in Charge, RCMP, Regina.

25. NAC RG10 v.6316 f.656-5 pt.7, 28 April 1947, Rev. Wickenden, Acting Principal, Gordon's Anglican Indian Residential School, Punnichy, Saskatchewan, to B.F. Neary, Superintendent of Welfare and Training, IAB, Ottawa.

26. NAC RG10 v.8754 f.651/25-1 pt.1, 19 November 1948, H.G. Buckle, Director of Corrections, Province of Saskatchewan, to J.P.B. Ostrander, Inspector of Indian Agencies, IAB, Regina.

27. NAC RG10 v.8754 f.651/25-1 pt.1, 1 March 1947, J.P.B. Ostrander, Inspector of Indian Agencies, IAB, Regina, to B.F. Neary, Superintendent of Training and Welfare, IAB, Ottawa.

28. Indeed, a brief submitted by the Anglican Church to a parliamentary committee in 1947 steadfastly defended the need for the half-day system of instruction at Indian residential schools whereby Indian children spent half of each school day performing chores related to the operation and maintenance of these institutions. See, ADSA, Box 55, 25 March 1947, a brief submitted by the Church of England in Canada to the Special Joint Committee of the Senate and House of Commons appointed to examine and consider the Indian Act.

29. NAC RG10 v.8754 f.651/25-1 pt.1, 16 May 1947, Director, Indian School Administration, MSCC, to R.A. Hoey, Director, IAB, Ottawa.

30. The camp was identified by federal authorities as Ex-122 Basic Training Camp. This particular location had been the site of the RCMP barracks until the mid-1930s.

31. NAC RG10 v.6322 f.658-5 pt.ll, 16 May 1947, B.F. Neary, Superintendent of Welfare and Training, IAB, to Crown Assets Allocation Committee, Ottawa.

32. Prior to his appointment to St. Alban's on 31 May 1947, Rev. Fisher had been the principal of the Anglican Indian residential school at Sioux Lookout in northern Ontario. See NAC RG10 v.6320 f.658-1 pt.2, 31 May 1947, Memo to the file, B.F. Neary, Superintendent of Welfare and Training, IAB, Ottawa.

33. The previous principal, the Rev. Ellis, left to become the chaplain at the federal penitentiary in Prince Albert.

34. NAC RG10 v.6323 f.658-6 pt.1, C.A.F. Clarke, IAB Educational Survey Officer, Report of Visit to St. Alban's Indian Residential School, 8–9 April 1947.

35. Ibid.

36. Ibid. The above cited remark would appear to suggest that IAB officials and residential school teachers did not expect Indian pupils to perform at the same level

as non-Indian children. This assumption represented a markedly different approach to Indian education than had been pursued at Emmanuel College. The remark also raises some important questions about the quality of the educational programs provided within Indian residential schools compared to those at other public schools.

37. NAC RG10 v.8754 f.651/25-1, pt.1, 28 November 1947, B.F. Neary, Superintendent of Welfare and Training, IAB, Ottawa, to J.P.B. Ostrander, Inspector of Indian Agencies, IAB, Regina.

38. NAC RG10 v.6323 f.658-10 pt.6, 12 December 1947, Rev. G.W. Fisher, Principal, St. Alban's, to Chief, Training Division, IAB, Ottawa.

39. NAC RG10 v.8754 f.651/25-1, pt.1, 3 May 1947, J.P.B. Ostrander, Regional Supervisor of Indian Agencies, IAB, Regina, to IAB, Ottawa.

40. Ibid.

41. The name "All Saints" had been used by the church to refer to the Indian residential school previously operated by the MSCC at Lac la Ronge. Although this name was used widely within Prince Albert to refer to the Anglican residential school established in the southwest part of the city, IAB officials in Ottawa continued to refer to the new facility as the "Lac la Ronge Indian Residential School in Prince Albert" even into the early 1960s.

42. NAC RG10 v.8754 f.651/25-1, pt.1, 21 May 1948, B.F. Neary, Superintendent of Indian Education, IAB, Ottawa, to J.P.B. Ostrander, Regional Supervisor of Indian Agencies, IAB, Regina.

43. NAC RG10 v.8754 f.651/25-1, pt.1, 5 June 1948, J.P.B. Ostrander, Regional Supervisor of Indian Agencies, IAB, Regina, to IAB, Ottawa. Note that the provincial government had already obtained use of one of the buildings at the site to house men taking provincially-sponsored vocational training in forestry work. Other buildings were being used by the Indian Health Service of the Department of National Health and Welfare and by the Carlton Agency of the IAB.

44. NAC RG10 v.6320 f.658-1 pt.2, 21 June 1948, J.P.B. Ostrander, Regional Supervisor of Indian Agencies, IAB, Regina, to IAB, Ottawa.

45. NAC RG10 v.8754 f.651/25-1, pt.1, 18 September 1948, B.F. Neary, Superintendent of Indian Education, IAB, Ottawa, to Rev. G.W. Fisher, Principal, St. Alban's, Prince Albert.

46. Ibid.

47. Ibid. It is also interesting to consider a report submitted by IAB personnel at the end of the school year in which they offered commendations to the matron of St. Alban's for the work done in "cleaning up and painting the interior of the school and in improving the appearance of the grounds" (NAC RG10 v.6323 f.658-6, pt.1, 19 June 1949, C.A.F. Clarke, IAB, Regina, Inspection Report for St. Alban's Indian Residential School, submitted to B.F. Neary, Superintendent of Indian Education, IAB, Ottawa). The question that arises is by whom was this work done. In view of the levels of staffing and shortage of funding that existed that year, it seems likely that these improvements were largely carried out by unpaid Indian pupils.

48. NAC RG10 v.8754 f.651/25-1, pt.1, 30 September 1948, Extract from Superintendent Jone's quarterly report for the period ended 30 September 1948.

49. NAC RG10 v.6323 f.658-10 pt.6, 21 October 1948, Rev. G.W. Fisher, Principal, St. Alban's, to the Superintendent, Indian Schools Administration, MSCC, Ottawa.

50. NAC RG10 v.8754 f.651/25-1, pt.1, 2 November 1948, C.A.F. Clarke, Educational

Survey Officer, IAB, Prince Albert, to the Superintendent of Indian Education, IAB, Ottawa.

51. John Tootoosis had been a prominent member of the League of Indians of Western Canada during the 1930s and was a well-known critic of Indian residential schools. See Sluman and Goodwill 1982:150; 180–81; 200.

52. Ibid.

53. Ibid.

54. The epidemic of mumps was followed by an outbreak of head lice.

55. NAC RG10 v.8754 f.651/25-1, pt.1, 4 November 1948, C.A.F. Clarke, Educational Survey Officer, IAB, Prince Albert, to Rev. G.W. Fisher, Principal, St. Alban's.

56. NAC RG10 v.6320 f.658-1 pt.2, 2 December 1948, J.P.B. Ostrander, Inspector of Indian Agencies, IAB, Regina, to B.F. Neary, Superintendent of Indian Education, IAB, Ottawa.

57. NAC RG10 v.6320 f.658-1 pt.2, 4 December 1948, Rev. G.W. Fisher, Principal, All Saints, to IAB, Ottawa.

58. NAC RG10 v.8754 f.651/25-1, pt.1, 14 December 1948, J.P.B. Ostrander, Regional Supervisor of Indian Agencies, IAB, Regina, to B.F. Neary, Supervisor of Indian Education, IAB, Ottawa.

59. Ibid.

60. These deficiencies were reported in an inspection conducted in October 1948. See NAC RG10 v.6322 f.658-5 pt.11, 23 March 1949, J.P.B. Ostrander, Regional Supervisor of Indian Agencies, IAB, Regina, to B.F. Neary, Supervisor of Indian Education, IAB, Ottawa.

61. Shirley Bear (1991: 44) remembers Rev. Scrase as "an angel. After he came, the whole system changed. He was just like a father to all the students."

62. I am grateful to Mr. Ernie Impey, a former long-time employee at All Saints and PAISEC for bringing this fact to my attention.

63. NAC RG10 v.6322 f.658-5 pt.11, 15 June 1949, E.S. Jones, Superintendent, Carlton Agency, Prince Albert, to IAB, Ottawa.

64. NAC RG10 v.8754 f.651/25-1, pt.1, 31 December 1949, Extract from Superintendent Jones' quarterly report for period ended 31 December 1949, Prince Alberta, submitted to IAB, Ottawa.

65. NAC RG10 v.8754 f.651/25-1, pt.1, 25 January 1950, J.P.B. Ostrander, Regional Supervisor of Indian Agencies, IAB, Regina, to IAB, Ottawa.

66. NAC RG10 v.8754 f.651/25-1, pt.1, 21 April 1950, C.A.F. Clarke, Educational Survey Officer, IAB, to Rev. A.J. Scrase, Principal, All Saints, Prince Albert.

67. NAC RG10 v.6323 f.658-6 pt.1, 14 February 1950, C.A.F. Clarke, Educational Survey Officer, IAB, to Rev. N.D. Pilcher, Principal, St. Alban's, Prince Albert.

68. NAC RG10 v.6323 f.658-6 pt.1, 25 May 1950, C.A.F. Clarke, Educational Survey Officer, IAB, to Superintendent of Indian Education, IAB, Ottawa.

69. NAC RG10 v.6323 f.658-6 pt.1, 7 June 1950, Rev. N.D. Pilcher, Principal, St. Alban's, to C.A.F. Clarke, Educational Survey Officer, IAB.

70. NAC RG10 v.6323 f.658-10 pt.6, 23 September 1950, Rev. H.G. Cook, Superintendent, Indian Schools Administration, MSCC, Ottawa, to B.F. Neary, Superintendent of Indian Education, IAB, Ottawa.

71. NAC RG10 v.6323 f.658-10 pt.6, 15 November 1950, Rev. N.D. Pilcher, Principal, St. Alban's, to Superintendent of the Carlton Agency, IAB, Prince Albert.

72. Ibid.

73. Ibid.
74. NAC RG10 v.8645 f.651/6-1 pt.1, 8 December 1950, B.F. Neary, Superintendent of Indian Education, IAB, Ottawa, Inspection Report for the Lac la Ronge [sic] Residential School.
75. An inspection of St. Alban's performed by a provincial government employee identified the following problems: inadequately-sized classrooms, inadequate blackboard space, a problem with noise, poor lighting and a lack of adequate tables. See NAC RG10 v.6323 f.658-6 pt.1, 10-11 May 1951, T.W. Waugh, Inspector of Schools, Report on St. Alban's School.
76. NAC RG10 v.8645 f.651/6-1 (1951-2) pt.1, 25 January 1951, Rev. H.G. Cook, Superintendent, ISA, MSCC, Ottawa, to B.F. Neary, Superintendent of Indian Education, IAB, Ottawa.
77. Ibid.
78. Ibid. See also ADSA, Box 53, Indian School Administration file, 2 May 1951, G.M.T. Hazen, Special Anglican Committee, Battleford, Saskatchewan, to Rev. Canon L.A. Dixon, General Secretary, MSCC, Toronto, for an outline of this proposal.

Chapter 4

On the Edge of the City
The Prince Albert Indian Residential School

The amalgamation of the St. Alban's and All Saints Indian residential schools into one institution in the fall of 1951 coincided with larger developments then unfolding within Canadian Indian administration. Revisions made to the Indian Act in 1951 served to eliminate some of the more obviously authoritarian and racist features of federal Indian administration such as the prohibition of the Sun Dance and Potlatch. By 1953 the Indian Affairs Branch had been transferred from the Department of Mines and Resources to the Department of Citizenship and Immigration. There was increasing recognition within government that existing levels of federal spending upon Indian education fell considerably short of being adequate—even with respect to the amount of food provided to pupils[1]—at a time when publicly-supported social, educational and health programs for other Canadians were being expanded in dramatic fashion. Yet while some additional resources were allocated to the Indian Affairs Branch, many premises and working practices of federal Indian administration remained unchanged. The principal objective of federal policy was to accomplish the cultural and economic integration of Indians into mainstream Canadian society at the least expense to the public purse. Officers of the Indian Affairs Branch, along with personnel from the various church bodies that operated Indian residential schools, continued to manage programs and make decisions on behalf of Indians. The bureaucratic presumption that Indian communities and families did not necessarily know what was in their best interests persisted.

In Prince Albert the amalgamation of two residential schools triggered a partial shift in relations between the Anglican Church and the Indian Affairs Branch. In previous years, when St. Alban's had operated in a building owned by the Diocese of Saskatchewan, federal officials had not hesitated to identify the structural shortcomings of that non-governmental facility. Now that the amalgamated school was fully housed on government property, there was a reversal of roles. Before the school re-opened at the former military base in the fall of 1951, officials of the MSCC called upon Ottawa to place the hastily constructed barracks buildings on concrete foundations, install interior sheathing and new roofs[2] to improve the appearance of the buildings and conserve heat, and supply an adequate fire alarm system at the school.[3] For their part, IAB officials criticized the church-employed school personnel who persisted in using the drill hall at the site not as a gymnasium but as a storage facility on the pretext that it was too expensive to heat the building during the winter.[4] The failure of the school to make use of the former drill hall for recreational purposes raised the possibility that some other government department might request use of the building from the Department of Public Works, thereby leaving the school without adequate indoor recreational facilities for Indian pupils during the winter months. In the view of regional IAB officials, the failure to make appropriate use of this building fell squarely on the shoulders of the church personnel:

> It is apparent from the attitude shown by the officials at this school that neither the church nor the school are interested in using the building for the purpose for which it was intended but prefer to use it for storage space for one truck, one tractor, and miscellaneous odds and ends that have accumulated. They have been using the building for this purpose for the past two years and have made no attempt to keep it clean or store materials in an orderly fashion. The doors are often left open and children from the school are allowed to roam about the building at will, wilfully damaging it without any interference from their supervisors. The latter statement is clearly illustrated by the fact that at least 180 window lights and about 1,000' of masonite have to be replaced if the building were renovated for a recreation hall.
>
> In an interview with the [school] staff some time last winter they collectively informed me that they had no time to supervise the children but after the interview several of them came to me separately each one explaining how hard he or she were trying to maintain discipline but how slack and lazy the others were.[5]

This particular issue illustrates a recurring organizational problem that plagued this and other residential schools. The joint operation of residential schools by churches and government fueled ongoing squabbling concerning the relative responsibilities of each side[6]. The funding of residential schools through per capita government grants inclined each partner to seek to keep its own expenditures and obligations to the minimum and to blame the other side when the shortcomings, inevitably generated by this strategy, eventually came to the surface. In this instance, insufficient supervisory staff at the school, along with the low grant provided for heating the school buildings, resulted in Indian pupils being denied use of an essential recreational facility for several years. Individual school and government personnel might have said that they were attempting to do the best that they could under the circumstances, however it should be noted that responsibility for the failure to establish satisfactory "circumstances" or identify the provision of appropriate standards of educational and child care services to Indian children as their top priority ultimately rested squarely on the shoulders of church and state. Indian families and bands had long been denied a voice in the operation of residential schooling, despite their informal efforts to monitor conditions within these institutions.

The Demand for Residential Schooling in Prince Albert

During its first month of operations in the fall of 1951 the newly amalgamated residential school in Prince Albert reported 436 pupils in attendance, even though its authorized pupilage had been set at 300.[7] The number of Indian children from northern Saskatchewan and parts of northern Manitoba who required residential schooling placed a serious load upon the capacity of the school. The school also suffered for some time from confusion about its name and location. As mentioned earlier, between 1948 and 1951 the temporary residential institution established at the former military base had been identified by IAB officials as the Lac la Ronge Indian Residential School in Prince Albert, while Anglican personnel had tended to identify it as All Saints, the church name that had been attached to the former residential school at Lac la Ronge. Following the 1951 amalgamation of St. Alban's and All Saints in Prince Albert, the principal of the new school had recommended that it be identified as the Prince Albert Indian Residential School (hereafter identified in this report as PAIRS) to avoid any confusion concerning the location of the school. Nevertheless, two years after the amalgamation he was still petitioning Ottawa to make this name change official in order to avoid the continuing problem of correspondence sent from IAB headquarters to the school being delivered to Lac la Ronge before it was redirected to Prince Albert.[8]

IAB personnel visited the school periodically, but the assessments of it submitted by individual bureaucrats varied substantially. In the fall of 1951 the local Indian agent reported a lack of discipline at the school and expressed concern regarding the principal's "haphazard and passive" approach.[9] A month later the regional Inspector of Indian Schools reported that the school supervisors at PAIRS were "people who should be properly qualified to supervise children."[10] In addition to commenting favourably upon the apparent level of interest shown by pupils in manual and domestic training courses, the inspector noted that the general condition of the dormitories was as good as could be expected in view of the leaky roofs, poor floors and need for redecoration of these buildings. An ostensibly unannounced visit to the school by the deputy minister in charge of the IAB in the late fall of 1952 left this senior official with a decidedly positive impression of PAIRS:

> As far as I know the staff and pupils had no advance notice of my visit. I visited the recreation hall and there I met the Supervisor of the sewing

room and some of the Indian girls working with her. Everyone appeared very interested in their work and I gathered the impression that the Supervisor, whose name I do not recall, had a gay personality which must be of great help in breaking the monotony of the work in that section. . . .

My general impression of the school was good. It is different from other residential schools and is more or less like a small village. I have been favourably impressed by the Principal [Rev. Scrase]. He looks interested in the welfare of the children and their education. I would say that he appears to be well liked by the Indian children if I judge by the way they smiled at him when we were visiting around. The children gave the impression of being well disciplined. Their morals appears [sic] to be good. The senior girls I met did not have that shyness complex which is often noticeable on some Indians.[11]

Notwithstanding this positive report by the deputy minister, inadequate funding for the school continued to pose problems for both church and branch officials, not to mention the children. For instance, when two pupils from northern Manitoba were allowed to go home in May 1953 to attend their father's funeral, their mother was expected to pay their return fares to Prince Albert so they might finish the school year.[12] Unable to meet this expense, she kept her children at home throughout the summer. In consequence, the government grant to the MSCC for the operation of PAIRS was accordingly reduced not only for the school days missed by these children in May and June but also for the vacation months of June and July, thereby prompting church officials to protest this loss of revenue. This matter and other tangled issues raised by the parsimonious per capita grant funding of residential schools occupied excessive amounts of time on the part of school and branch officials. Moreover, the perennial scarcity of funding for anything beyond a bare minimum level of residential school operations meant that most Indian pupils and their families were either effectively denied access to one another during the school year or were expected to cover the costs of any travel necessitated by family emergencies. What was more, at a time when the merit of maintaining agriculture operations in conjunction with Indian residential schools was being questioned, the Anglican church still insisted that the school farm operated at Prince Albert on six acres of rented land was essential to the operations of PAIRS since it provided a significant proportion of the food served at the school.[13] In the case of Prince Albert the MSCC called for the potato, carrot and turnip acreage to be tripled. The school possessed its own tractor and potato digger, and there was no shortage of children who could be called on to pick potatoes and harvest other vegetables.

Another chronic problem at PAIRS involved the disrepair of buildings that had originally been constructed for short-term use during the war. By 1954 the deterioration of the huts that housed the school had reached a point that obliged branch officials to consider making expensive repairs, reducing the size of the school significantly or even closing it altogether.[14] Consultations conducted within the branch indicated that it would have been politically inexpedient to close one of two Anglican residential schools in Saskatchewan while seven Roman Catholic residential schools remained in the province.[15] Moreover, the rapid growth in the population of school-aged Indian children was creating logistical difficulties for federal schooling programs across Canada. Prince Albert was viewed as being the logical location for a Protestant residential school, but the cost of building an entirely new school building there for 300 children was thought to be beyond the budget of the branch at that time.[16] Financial considerations dictated that the school would remain within "army hut buildings" that would be refurbished to accommodate 300 pupils rather than the almost 500 children then attending PAIRS. It was hoped that for a total cost of $140,000 the life of the facility could be extended for some ten to fifteen years.[17]

Almost as soon as these plans had been adopted they began to be modified, and by July 1954 the Prince Albert school authorities were preparing for the fall enrolment of 450 pupils. Indian day labourers were hired to begin work on remodelling the dormitories, but a contractor retained to undertake the main part of the work was a month late in starting the job. The fall term at the school was chaotic with some 350 children having to be sent home for lack of finished accommodation.[18] Poor weather and difficulties in obtaining construction supplies further lengthened the project. Even before the renovations began in earnest, the MSCC had reported that the Prince Albert Indian Residential School was running at a deficit due to the high cost of heating the dispersed and inadequately insulated huts.[19] With the drastic drop in per capita grant funding caused by construction delays the MSCC insisted that the federal government retire the accumulated school operating deficit and temporarily abandon its funding formula to pay the actual costs of operating the school until the renovations were finished.[20]

By the end of the 1954–55 school year attendance at PAIRS averaged approximately 300 pupils.[21] A year later it was upgraded to an authorized pupilage of 350 children and reported an actual average attendance of 378 pupils, making it the second largest Indian residential school in Canada.[22] As IAB officials noted, the denominational agencies managing residential schools regularly made supplemental requests to cover the costs of educating more children than permitted by terms of the schools' authorized pupilage, so it was not the case that the churches were educating these children "for free."[23]

An examination of the records of pupil admission and discharge to the Prince Albert Indian Residential School between 1955 and 1957 shows that children at the school came from reserves and Indian communities across Saskatchewan as well as from out of province. Pupils' home communities included: White Bear, The Pas, Mistawasis, Mosquito-Grizzly Bear Head, Red Pheasant, Sandy Lake, Gordon's, Shoal Lake, Cote, Aklavik (Fort Norman Agency, NWT), Peepeekisis,

James Smith, Moosomin, Little Pine, Sweet Grass, Key, Lac La Ronge, Sturgeon Lake, Churchill (Manitoba), John Smith, Peter Ballantyne, Ochapowace, Red Earth, William Charles (Montreal Lake) and White Cap's.[24] The children living in residence ranged from six to eighteen years of age and, though mostly Anglican, there were also pupils whose parents' religious affiliation was identified as United Church or Presbyterian.[25] While considerable care was taken to ensure that denominational boundaries were observed, children with one Roman Catholic parent and one Protestant parent were sometimes admitted. A parent or guardian was normally requested to sign an application for admission.[26]

Since there were always many more applicants to PAIRS than there was space to accommodate them, the IAB Superintendent of Education in Ottawa scrutinized all applications and referred a significant proportion of these back to local agency superintendents (also known as Indian agents) to ensure that individual applicants would be unlikely to obtain an education unless they attended the Prince Albert Indian Residential School. Acceptable reasons for IAB personnel recommending admission to PAIRS included a lack of accessible educational facilities in local communities and a broad range of social considerations. The following represents a cross-section of "reasons for recommending admission" entered by local IAB personnel on individual application forms submitted to PAIRS during the mid-1950s:

- To attend high school;
- [Home] Too far from school;
- Overcrowded condition of Moose Woods day school;
- Child rather backward. Father requests one or two years at Residential School for closer supervision;
- Mother in P.A. Sanitarium. Father unable to care for them. Grandparents . . . caring for child;
- Father is in hospital;
- Due to very unsatisfactory conditions at home, this girl has been brought in to the Residential School;
- The child lives 2 1/2 miles from school and is too small to go to school alone and the parents are moving out of the Reserve to seek employment elsewhere;
- This child baptized Catholic—parents were Catholic. Mother states they are no longer Catholic but are free Methodist and wish the girl to go to Prince Albert School;
- Living conditions on the reserve are very far from Satisfactory, as the mother is not able to care for them and the foster home is not good. Mother in asylum, parents separated;
- Mother is in hospital most of the time. Father away trapping. Balance of children are at above school;

- Mother is dead and the father does not provide a home for this boy;
- The Red Earth Indian Day School is very much overcrowded;
- This child's progress in school has been slow and quite backward. It is felt that this boy would benefit by spending some of his school years at the P.A. Residential School;
- . . . is well up with her work, even if she has had a struggle with English. She is a conscientious student and is very determined;
- Father away trapping most of the time. Dr. . . . of Indian Health Services advises the mother is not at all well and is going mental and cannot cope with the above child or look after her properly;
- No school available;
- Widow, destitute;
- The parents are on a trapline . . . where there is no school available;
- Parents out on trap line all winter;
- . . . wishes to have a high school education and intends to enter the dental profession if his marks are high enough;
- The school situated on the Reserve is not within reasonable distance;
- Parents do not live together. Child raised by . . . grandfather;
- Parents deserted this child and grandmother is raising it now;
- Broken home. Parents of child are separated. Child kept by mother;
- No grade eight pupils in Day School on Reserve;
- Mother in sanitarium. [Father] finds it impossible to care for these children;
- . . . polio. Should be encouraged to attend high school;
- Broken home. Mother unable to support child;
- This woman [the mother] recently discharged from Saskatchewan Hospital. Unable to care for child;
- Father of children is dead. Mother has no means of support;
- This child is an orphan and I recommend that she be admitted in order that she may take the higher grades;
- This girl has been living in a private home, but the parents are finding it difficult to pay for her maintenance . . . ;
- To attend Prince Albert Residential School and study at Prince Albert Collegiate . . . ;
- Parents have been separated for some years. Home life not too satisfactory;
- Do not teach Grade nine at the Pas Indian Day School;
- Mother's health poor, unable to take charge, large family;
- Parents nomadic, living off of reserve;
- Father not interested in welfare of his children (some chief). House and home just a hovel. Student should be away from present environment. Mother does try to see that the children get an education.[27]

Clearly, by the mid-1950s PAIRS was being used by the federal government to serve substantial child welfare and social development purposes as well as educational functions.

Alarmed by rising enrolments across the country, federal officials began to rethink the role of residential schools within the overall field of Indian education. To limit enrolment and, thereby, the operational costs of residential schooling, the federal government articulated a policy that called for: (1) admitting to residential schools only those children who required institutional care for social or family reasons along with children living in communities without school facilities; (2) opening more day schools on reserves and improving local transportation access to these schools; and (3) subsidizing the enrolment of Indian children into non-Indian schools.[28] The new criteria for admission to residential schools were expected to exist particularly in northern regions,[29] and elsewhere the branch hoped to relieve the demand for Indian education through an "integration" program, although federal officials denied that it would be synonymous with "assimilation."[30] There was also interest in the churches possibly helping to locate suitable boarding homes for Indian children who travelled to non-Indian communities for secondary education.

The promotion of integrated schooling by federal officials in the postwar period represented a fundamental shift both in the management of Indian education and the future administration of Indian affairs in Canada. Since Confederation this had been the only educational field over which the federal government had exercised jurisdiction. Yet from the commencement of federal funding of Indian residential schooling in the early 1880s, federal officials had opted to maintain constitutional control over Indian education by means of partnerships with religious denominations. Churches were seen as possessing the moral authority and educational expertise required to operate schools. By the end of the Second World War, however, the underlying structural and financial problems that had long plagued the working relationship between church and state in administering Indian education prompted a far-reaching reassessment of this arrangement.[31] Proposals to transfer some Indian children to schools in provincial educational systems involved a surrender of federal jurisdiction over Indian education. In the short run this measure offered the Indian Affairs Branch an alternative to constructing many new schools to accommodate increases in both Indian population growth and more systematic enrolment of all Indian children in schooling. In the longer term, however, integrated schooling was the first administrative step in what would become a piecemeal but ongoing transfer of governmental jurisdiction over Indians and Indian lands to provincial governments. While federal officials did consult with church and provincial educational officials about the integrated schooling program, virtually no effort was made to consult Aboriginal peoples about this fundamental shift at the time this policy was adopted.

To make the prospect of enrolling Indian pupils in provincial schools more

Emmanuel College, August 1891
(Anglican Diocese of Saskatchewan Archives)

Students and staff in front of new building, Emmanuel College, early 1900s
(Anglican Diocese of Saskatchewan Archives)

Students, staff and guests, Emmanuel College, early 1900s
(Canada, Sessional Papers, 1905)

Girls of the graduating class, All Saints, 1950 (Mrs. Bernice Logan)

Getting ready for a picnic, All Saints, 1950 (Mrs. Bernice Logan)

Row of dormitory huts at All Saints campus, 1950 (Mrs. Bernice Logan)

Residential school farmer and students, All Saints, 1949 (Mrs. Bernice Logan)

Prince Albert Midget Hockey Champions, All Saints hockey team
with Rev. Scrase, 1950 (Mrs. Bernice Logan)

Benny, a young student at
All Saints, 1950
(Mrs. Bernice Logan)

Percy Bear, heading home on the school truck
from All Saints for summer holidays, 1949
(Mrs. Bernice Logan)

Primary grades classroom at All Saints, 1950 (Mrs. Bernice Logan)

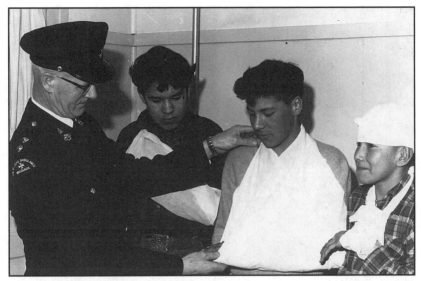

St. John's Ambulance junior nursing program for boys, Prince Albert Indian Residential School, March 1962 (Prince Albert Historical Society)

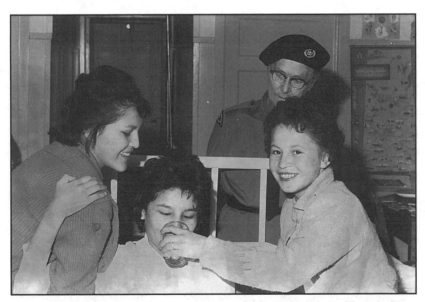

St. John's Ambulance junior nursing program for girls, Prince Albert Indian Residential School, March 1962 (Prince Albert Historical Society)

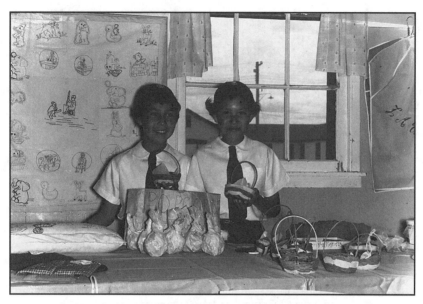

Selling candy at a tea and bazaar, Prince Albert Indian Residential School, June 1965 (Prince Albert Historical Society)

Santa Claus at the Prince Albert Indian Residential School, December 1966 (Prince Albert Historical Society)

Students arriving at the Prince Albert Indian Student Education Centre,
August 1995 (PAISEC)

Bingo Night at PAISEC, Fall 1995 (PAISEC)

Waiting for a school bus, PAISEC, Winter 1995–96 (PAISEC)

Crosswalk patrol for children returning to PAISEC campus from Angus Mirasty School, Fall 1995 (PAISEC)

attractive to local school boards, the federal government proposed not only to pay per capita grants to these authorities but also to provide capital construction funds to enlarge their facilities.[32] The integration program proceeded upon the assumption that the educational requirements and social and cultural needs of Indian children could be satisfied as well as or perhaps better in provincial non-Indian schools than in federal educational institutions. The possibility that Indian children might be subjected to educational administrators, instructors and non-Indian classmates who might view and treat them as being racially and culturally inferior to other Canadians did not seem to trouble or even occur to federal officials. It was simply taken for granted that it was in the best interests of Indians for the government to adopt such a policy unilaterally. Nonetheless, branch officials were instructed to exercise caution in introducing individual integrated or "joint" school agreements and to establish band school committees both to facilitate acceptance of joint schooling agreements and develop "a sense of responsibility in the adult Indian."[33] Indian parents and leaders, who had long been systematically excluded from decision-making processes concerning their children's education, had come to be defined in the bureaucratic mind as lacking a "sense of responsibility."

By 1958 the Indian Affairs Branch's national educational programs had changed substantially in form and scale from what had existed ten years earlier.[34] Between 1947 and 1958 the number of Indian pupils in Canada doubled.[35] Moreover, during the same period the number of Indian children enrolled in non-Indian schools had gone from 200 to more than 7,000 since the late 1940s. These integrated or joint schooling arrangements had been cautiously advocated by departmental officials as the form of schooling best-suited to succeed denominationally-operated residential schools. In response, certain church officials, including the Bishop of Saskatchewan, had argued the case for maintaining church-operated residential schools:

> These Residential Schools provide the Church with a unique opportunity of inculcating in the minds of the Indian boys and girls the tenets of our faith. They should be used as training institutions, not only for the purpose of sending out the young Indian equipt to live in the white man's world, but also fully equipt as a well established Christian boy or girl. These Schools should be something more than institutions, they should be homes. . . .[36]

Nonetheless, by the early 1950s, widespread criticism of Indian residential schooling had prompted even the Indian Schools Administration of the Anglican Church to take a more conciliatory stance with respect to integrated schooling proposals and to acknowledge that residential schools might comprise only a phase in the long-term evolution of Indian education.[37] The curriculum of residential schools was transformed accordingly during the

1950s, with the traditional "half-day" system (in which children spent four hours or fewer each weekday in classes and the rest of their time working on farm or domestic chores) being replaced by full-day school programs. By the late 1950s residential schools were also increasingly used to accommodate children who could not be adequately cared for in their home communities due to domestic or other social factors.

Nonetheless, the pressure to admit additional pupils to the Prince Albert Indian Residential School rose steadily. By 1957 the authorized pupilage for the institution had been raised to 367, but actual attendance stood at 382.[38] Regional IAB officials reported that this overenrolment had occurred in spite of the fact that the school had sent home a considerable number of children who would otherwise have enrolled in grade one.[39] An increasing proportion of the children housed at the residence were attending high school in the city, for PAIRS had only ever offered classes from grades one to eight. In 1957 IAB officials approached the Prince Albert School Board to ask that new public schools constructed in the city accommodate Indian children in grades seven and eight as well as secondary school students. The following year an agreement was negotiated to have educated in city schools all Indian children above grade six who were residing at PAIRS.[40]

Demand for space at PAIRS continued to exceed supply, especially since federal authorities thought it impractical to construct day schools in several northern communities. Notwithstanding the shortage of space at the residence, the MSCC identified a strong need "to provide reception rooms where visiting Indian parents could meet and talk with their children instead of having to visit them in their dormitories."[41] Extra-curricular activities for pupils housed at the residence included sports and Air Cadets.[42] The school principal carefully monitored and directly paid incidental high school fees charged for books, examinations, school sports participation and graduation ceremonies.[43] While older Indian students were provided with small allowances to cover expenditures for personal grooming in an attempt to bridge the gap between them and non-Indian students in city schools, the propriety of even this inexpensive measure concerned federal officials. At a 1960 Ottawa meeting with Anglican Indian residential school principals, IAB representatives accepted the wisdom of providing Indian pupils who were attending non-Indian schools with such allowances but contended that public funds ought not to be used for this purpose; in their view, the church ought to have funded all personal allowances.[44] Evidently, federal authorities were determined to maintain a distinction between necessary expenditures and what they feared might be viewed as acts of charity in the operation of Indian residential schools.

At the same meeting the emergence of a number of other common operational problems was noted. Although teachers and other classroom personnel had been employed directly by IAB since 1954, dormitory supervisors and other residence personnel at Anglican institutions remained direct employees of the Indian

Schools Administration of the MSCC.[45] Not only had difficulties been encountered in matching the title and duties of dormitory supervisors with emerging labour standards, but also most residence supervisors were said to be working many more hours for much lower wages than was permitted under existing regulations. Although IAB grants to the MSCC were calculated at the basis of one dormitory supervisor for every thirty pupils, the implementation of the integrated or joint schooling program meant that children were daily away from residences for hours at a time and, thus, were unable to perform many of the domestic chores that they had traditionally done. The increased use of residential schools to house Indian children admitted for various social reasons also augmented the proportion of pupils exhibiting behavioural problems, thereby adding to the challenges confronting supervisory personnel. It was the feeling of the principals that some local Indian agents were intentionally sending troubled children out of reserve communities and into the residential schools.[46] Staffing levels were plainly inadequate to cope with the evolving requirements of residential schooling in Prince Albert.

Increasing Responsibilities and Deteriorating Buildings

At PAIRS these operational problems were further compounded by the shortcomings of the buildings at the facility. The original decision to make use of the former military camp sought to minimize government expenditures. Although the renovations made to the campus in 1954 had been intended to extend the life of the facility for ten to fifteen years, by 1960 the campus had become decidedly shoddy in appearance. Rev. Bramwell, the principal, asked his superiors to press federal officials concerning how much longer these "temporary" buildings were going to be considered "permanent":

> For instance, the staff sitting room is anything but attractive and no amount of paint will make it so as the wall board is bulging and a host of pipes run across the ceiling. Then too the staff have to take their meals at one end of the children's dining room—anything but an attractive room.
>
> To my mind, the outworn appearance of the whole school interior has a depressing effect on pupils and . . . [staff] alike.[47]

Rev. Bramwell sent photographs of staff accommodation to Ottawa to demonstrate the poor condition of the housing provided for the school's dormitory supervisors.[48] IAB officials in Ottawa acknowledged the deterioration of living conditions at the school by reducing the payroll deduction for accommodation charged to PAIRS staff members,[49] although no similar form of discount or compensation for enduring poor housing conditions was extended to the pupils.

When the Saskatchewan Anti-Tuberculosis League announced its intention to close its sanitarium in Prince Albert, Rev. Bramwell proposed to Ottawa that this building might, with some modifications, be suitable as a replacement facility for PAIRS.[50] Although a refurbished sanitarium would hold only 300 children, Bramwell judged that this measure would cost far less than the $1 million estimated to rebuild PAIRS on its existing site. He also observed that city officials coveted the land on which PAIRS was located and resented the continuing operation of a residential school there. So, with an eye toward both obtaining an improved school facility and enhancing community relations, Bramwell recommended moving PAIRS to the former "San."

Federal officials had been aware of the City of Prince Albert's interest in obtaining the residence lands for some time[51] and had taken account of a spate of locally-generated "complaints" about Indian students' behaviour. In the short run Ottawa would recommend that meetings be held in Prince Albert between Indian school staff members and community representatives to find way of improving relationships between the school and the community. Instructions were also issued to the school authorities:

> Institute a carefully planned program at the school to encourage and enforce exemplary behaviour on the part of Indian children in their contacts with the community. This should include extra class activities that will promote goodwill and understanding between Indian and non-Indian children.
>
> Sternly eradicate any elements of the school which tend to set up tensions between the school and the community.[52]

Exactly what such "eradication" might entail and which "elements" were to be targeted were not specified, but the federal government was committed to maintaining a residential facility for Indian children somewhere in Prince Albert so that it might make use of space in city schools as a means of forestalling the costs of providing full elementary and secondary school programs in Indian communities. What was more, both the Prince Albert School Board and the local Chamber of Commerce were eager to extend the use of the city's educational facilities to Indian students in return for federal funding.[53] From the local perspective, negotiating a larger share of the expanding federal budget for Indian education offered local rate-payers an attractive means of subsidizing the construction of new and better equipped schools for their own children.[54] Every federal dollar spent on behalf of Indian children in local schools would be a dollar that would not have be to raised in the form of taxes upon Prince Albert property owners. The question that remained, however, was whether Indian children would be as welcome in local schools as were federal dollars.

By 1961 departmental decisions that PAIRS would remain where it was and that integrated schooling would be extended to Indian elementary students in grades beneath grade seven prompted Rev. Bramwell to identify a number of logistical problems that were likely to ensue.[55] Although Bramwell declared himself sympathetic to the purposes of the integration program and agreed that Indian children attending city schools should not form large and unassimilable groups, he was concerned about the plan to have small numbers of Indian children in each grade distributed across six local schools. This would raise problems for residence supervisors in keeping track of children on their way to and from different schools and would also oblige PAIRS to obtain an additional vehicle to provide transportation. He noted the inability of either the junior boys supervisor (who was responsible for overseeing fifty-four pupils) or the girls supervisor (who was responsible for forty-eight children) to monitor the movement of children several times daily across main roads and a provincial highway. Nor did the schooling agreement make provision for supplying midday meals to Indian students or noon-hour supervision. Finally, Bramwell doubted that the proposal to dispatch Indian children to city schools whenever and wherever space became available would be beneficial for these children:

> The proposed scheme is not integration in its true or best sense but it is rather a matter of filling the vacant places which exist for this year and gives no premise of continuity and from our previous experiences (grades 7 & 8) is likely to mean a change of schools for students which is likely to make children feel that they are indeed different from the white children.
>
> Proper integration requires that there should be continuity, this essentially requires that there should be an arrangement where approximately the same number of children should be in each grade; that is the children would naturally follow through the grades in the school concerned.
>
> The proposed scheme is a filling of vacancies with no certainty of a continuing progress through school . . . .[56]

Previous experience led the principal to predict that extending the integration program to younger children would engender a greater incidence of truancy. Any chance for successful implementation of this particular arrangement for integrated schooling in Prince Albert would, Bramwell calculated, require at least five additional staff members at PAIRS and other expenditures to support the scheme. IAB officials were inclined to view Bramwell's concerns as being exaggerated, noting that his tendency in managing PAIRS was to exercise a more tightly controlled and disciplined institution than was the case in other residential schools where the integration program had been implemented.

As well as forcing integrated schooling upon an increasing proportion of PAIRS pupils, Ottawa officials introduced a boarding home policy that was designed to redirect some of the older children attending residential schools to alternative forms of placement.[57] Whereas residential schools were increasingly being used to serve orphans, children from broken homes, and others for whom child welfare considerations were a primary concern, the boarding home program was not intended to provide foster home care. Although children sent to residential schools or foster homes were legally subjected to the guardianship of the school principal or welfare authorities for the duration of their stay, the placement of Indian children in boarding homes would not involve a transfer of guardianship:

> parental consent in writing must be obtained before any placement can be made by Branch officials who are merely acting on behalf of the parents to ensure the child's educational progress. Accordingly, parents are expected to make the maximum contribution to the cost of the programme for their respective children.[58]

Some Indian homes might be included in this program but the majority of boarding homes were expected to be provided by non-Indian families. The use of the boarding home program in Prince Albert for students in grades eleven and twelve was intended to relieve at least some of the demand for accommodation at the residence.[59]

From Huts to Cottages

In 1962 the branch finally decided to reconstruct the Prince Albert Indian Residential School at its existing site through replacement of huts with a number of twenty-four-pupil cottages rather than a single large dormitory.[60] Preliminary plans called for accommodation for at least 350 children and, depending upon how the local school integration program proceeded, possibly a six-classroom block for educating primary students on campus rather than in city schools. Phased construction of the cottages over a period of three to five years would entail certain limitations but would also serve to spread out capital construction costs over a number of years.[61] Commencement of the construction project was, however, delayed until the 1964–65 fiscal year due to the imposition of a federal government austerity program. Anglican representatives contacted the Minister of Citizenship and Immigration during this period to ensure that the project would, in fact, be carried out.[62] Indeed, the commitment made by federal officials was firmly incorporated into the IAB's capital estimates, for this particular federal government construction project happened to be located in the constituency of then Prime Minister John Diefenbaker.

IAB design and construction officials put much care and initiative into drawing up plans for the PAIRS reconstruction project. The decision to rebuild a number of small cottages served not only to retain the distinctive nature of the PAIRS campus relative to other residential school facilities but also to inspire the designers to envision additional facilities including even a motel that would accommodate visiting officials and parents. What was sought was a less institutional and more "homey" atmosphere that would be welcoming to pupils

76

and staff alike.[63] Visits to a similar school campus in the United States and two residential facilities operated for non-Indian children in Ontario allowed IAB staff to check their designs for PAIRS against comparable institutions.[64] Branch officials calculated that they would be able to provide modern residential cottages at PAIRS for approximately half the cost of construction incurred at one of the Ontario institutions and about two-thirds the cost of a large centralized dormitory building of the type usually designed by the Department of Public Works for this purpose.[65]

Although the PAIRS project proceeded with an uncommon degree of enthusiasm on the part of IAB technical officials, the traditional emphasis placed upon keeping costs down was not entirely abandoned. In the end, the plans for the redevelopment were scaled down. A chapel, separate housing for the principal and vice-principal, separate medical and administrative buildings, and the school classrooms were deleted from the project. Nevertheless, the construction of new cottage dormitories and the erection of a new building that combined food services, medical services and administrative offices represented a significant federal investment in the provision of residential accommodation, if not of schooling, in Prince Albert. Having figuratively dug into the site on a long-term basis, IAB officials steadfastly resisted a request from the City of Prince Albert to extend 22nd Street West through the centre of the PAIRS campus in order to open up an east-west arterial route that would permit further housing development in the West Hill area of the city.[66] They were, however, prepared to share the northwest corner of the site when the RCMP requested clearance to relocate its Prince Albert facilities to where these had originally been situated from the 1880s until the 1930s.[67]

The provision of new buildings and the commitment of design personnel to a "family-like situation" at the residence did not, however, resolve all operational problems at PAIRS. Indeed, the designers' plan to have twelve girls and twelve boys in each cottage raised questions about the need for male and female supervisory staff in each cottage, giving rise to the suggestion that married couples might provide an appropriate means for accomplishing this.[68] But this arrangement prompted further questions about how much each member of a supervisory couple would be paid and whether residence employees would be prepared to work as long hours for as little pay as they had done in the past as church employees. In the shorter run, the phasing in of new dormitories had apparently undermined staff harmony since those supervisors appointed to the new cottages had fewer children to oversee than did their counterparts in the remaining army huts.[69] This disparity of work loads among staff members, along with increased competition for the services of good staff members from provincial institutions that offered five-day, forty-hour work weeks with relatively high salaries, prompted local IAB officials reluctantly to recommend increased levels of staffing at PAIRS.[70]

Rethinking Residential Schooling: The Caldwell Report

Shortly after the PAIRS reconstruction program commenced, the newly established Department of Indian Affairs and Northern Development (DIAND) commissioned a research study in 1967 of the child care programs of nine residential schools operating in Saskatchewan (Caldwell 1967). Highlighting some of the common deficiencies of residential schooling, the report noted the confusion within these institutions concerning their mandate as denominational missions, educational facilities or child welfare centres (Caldwell 1967:2). In fact, almost 60 percent of pupils admitted to residential schools in Saskatchewan in 1965–66 were there for social rather than purely educational reasons (Caldwell 1967:62–64), since, in the absence of federal child welfare services for Indian children, residential schools had been used for a variety of social development purposes, including that of resolving situations where children were deemed to be in need of protection (Caldwell 1967:66).

George Caldwell, the professional social worker who authored the study, observed that:

> Professional services in the institution[s] to help children modify or resolve their behaviour and personality problems are completely lacking. This is not intended to reflect on principals, teachers or clergy in the schools, but to stress the point that in the functions which they primarily discharge they are neither equipped nor should they be expected to provide professional casework service. (1967:67)

In Caldwell's view the separation of responsibilities between church authorities and federal officials in the operation of residential schools had become quite problematic. The churches' financial contributions to the operation of residential schools were minimal, and the study found that the children surveyed placed little significance upon the religious component of their experience in residential schools (Caldwell 1967:36). Caldwell also found that the cost to the federal government of operating residential schools was low in comparison with most progressive institutional programs for providing social development and child welfare services precisely because of a departmental philosophy of caring for Indian children "at the least public expense rather than developing a program to meet the special needs of children, which will cost considerably more" (1967:92).

The vast majority of children surveyed by members of the study team indicated that they desired greater interaction with their parents (Caldwell 1967:24). Most children attended residential school for ten months of the year, returning home for the summer holidays and sometimes for the Christmas vacation, although parents were expected to contribute towards transportation costs incurred during this holiday season (Caldwell 1967:104). Caldwell observed that while residential school staff members did not express overt hostility towards Indian parents, they seemed to him to share a conviction that visits by parents to the schools upset the children and the routine of the system (1967:105). At the time of the study less than a quarter of residential school staff members were Indians, and most of those were employed in housekeeping and maintenance positions. Less than 20 percent of all Indian employees were child care workers (Caldwell 1967:113). More than half of the non-teaching employees of the residential schools responding to the study did not have high school education (Caldwell 1967:122).

In Caldwell's opinion a wide gap separated PAIRS from all other institutions examined in the study. As well as being the largest residential school in Saskatchewan and architecturally distinct, it was the only one located in an urban area. PAIRS had by 1966 enrolled almost two-thirds of its pupils (i.e., all pupils above the grade five level) in joint or integrated schooling arrangements in Prince Albert; they represented over 80 percent of all Saskatchewan residential school students in integrated school programs (Caldwell 1967:81). In general terms Caldwell appeared to prefer the operations of PAIRS to those of other schools included in the study, although he identified it as one which employed a more authoritarian line in dealing with children.[71] Overall, he termed the disciplinary problems reported by the schools as being "minimal" and, perhaps, even "disturbingly low" compared to those experienced in non-Indian residential institutions for children (Caldwell 1967:109–10).

Caldwell's report concluded that residential schools in Saskatchewan had come to provide service in custodial care rather than child development. He recommended that the churches remove themselves from this field: "The involvement of the churches in the residential school field has become so systematized that it has become a managerial function rather than a creative and dynamic force for change" (Caldwell 1967:152). He further recommended that the federal government concern itself with the education of Indian children and discontinue the operation of residential schools as child welfare institutions. If Indian children needed to leave home to continue their education for any reason, Caldwell suggested they be housed in Indian and white foster homes, transition homes designed to help children assimilate from Indian to white culture, or in hostels designed to provide group care for Indian children in urban settings (Caldwell 1967:153). His recommendations reflected some popular administrative beliefs and assumptions of that period. He accepted without question that integrated schooling programs were in the best interests of Indian children, a view that had been firmly held by federal officials since at least the early 1950s. He assumed that the provision of adequate child welfare and social development services to Indian children and families would be best delivered not by church or federal authorities but by provincial agencies. Finally, while noting the manner in which Indian parents had been systematically separated from the development of residential school children, Caldwell did not call for greater involvement by Indian families and communities in charting the future course of these and other aspects of Indian education.

Caldwell's 1967 report was highly influential within federal government circles. Its call for an end to church involvement in residential schooling was necessitated in 1969 when it was determined that all non-teaching residential school staff would become federal employees. Notwithstanding the clear thinking that underpinned many of his criticisms, Caldwell's final recommendations for improving the treatment of Indian children were in keeping with the sentiments that shaped the 1969 federal government proposals concerning the future of Indian administration. What was more, his report indirectly endorsed the course of action that had been taken in Prince Albert where a residential school was being systematically transformed into a residence or hostel facility.

The announcement of the federal government's takeover of the Indian residences and hostels across Canada on April 1, 1969 prompted a flurry of action on the part of a number of church leaders in a last-minute attempt to reverse or modify the decision.[72] The Bishop of Saskatchewan contacted John Diefenbaker, the MP for Prince Albert and former prime minister, asking that he raise questions in the House of Commons concerning the proposed transfer. Bemoaning the loss of influence that the churches would suffer, the bishop nonetheless claimed that what concerned him most was "the fact that the Indian people have not been consulted nor informed of this very drastic move on the part of the Department of Indian Affairs."[73] Minister of Indian and Northern Affairs, Jean Chretien, countered this line of argument with the claim that since the decision involved "a purely administrative claim, it was not felt necessary to discuss the matter with the Indians."[74] The minister did, however, indicate that the churches would be asked to nominate individuals for the position of administrator at each residence and would in this way continue to exercise influence over the choice of child care workers. Also, the federal government undertook to pay the Diocese of Saskatchewan a fee of $3,500 per annum in return for providing chaplaincy services for Indian pupils at the residence in Prince Albert.[75]

Notes

1 . In the fall of 1951 an IAB official reported to his superiors the findings of a detailed internal study of two Indian residential schools in northern Ontario. The study determined that the government had not provided sufficient funding to enable the church administrators to offer adequate meals or clothing to the pupils enrolled there. There is no indication that this internal report had been or would be publicized. See NAC RG10 v.8797 f.1/25-13-1, 20 October 1951, C.A.F. Clarke, Educational Survey Officer, IAB, to Superintendent of Education, IAB, Ottawa.

2. NAC RG10 v.8645 f.651/6-1 (1951-52) pt.1, 20 June 1951a, Rev. H.G. Cook, Superintendent, Indian Schools Administration, MSCC, Ottawa, to P.N. Phelan, Superintendent of Indian Education, IAB, Ottawa.

3. NAC RG10 v.8645 f.651/6-1 (1951-52) pt.1, 20 June 1951b, Rev. H.G. Cook, Superintendent, Indian Schools Administration, MSCC, Ottawa, to P.N. Phelan, Superintendent of Indian Education, IAB, Ottawa.

4   NAC RG10 v.8645 f.651/6-1 (1951-52) pt.1, 9 August 1951, D.N. Morrison, Supervisor of Construction, IAB, Regina, to J.P.B. Ostrander, Regional Supervisor of Indian Agencies, IAB, Regina.

5. Ibid.

6. See NAC RG10 v.8797 f.1/25-13-1, 20 October 1951, C.A.F. Clarke, Educational Survey Officer, IAB, to Superintendent of Education, IAB, Ottawa, for an admission by an IAB official of the manner in which the federal government had systematically minimized funding to the church bodies on the expectation that the churches would acquire second-hand clothing for Indian children through charitable donations.

7. See NAC RG10 v.8754 f.651/25-1, 13 August 1952, P. Phelan, Superintendent of Education, IAB, Ottawa, to J.P.B. Ostrander, Regional Supervisor of Indian Agencies, IAB, Regina.

8. NAC RG10 v.8754 f.651/25-1, 23 June 1953, Rev. H.G. Cook, Superintendent of the ISA, MSCC, Ottawa, to P.N. Phelan, Superintendent of Education, IAB, Ottawa. The branch subsequently acceded, albeit grudgingly, to the principal's request; see NAC RG10 v.8754 f.651/25-1, 7 July 1953, H.M. Jones, Acting Director, IAB, Ottawa, to Deputy Minister, Department of Citizenship and Immigration.

9. NAC RG10 v.8754 f.651/25-1, 2 November 1951, P. Phelan, Superintendent of Education, IAB, Ottawa, to J.P.B. Ostrander, Regional Supervisor of Indian Agencies, IAB, Regina.

10. NAC RG10 v.8754 f.651/25-1, 11 December 1951, Inspection Report, R.N. Conrad, Regional Inspector of Indian Schools, IAB, Saskatchewan.

11. NAC RG10 v.8754 f.651/25-1, 6 December 1952, L. Fortier, Deputy Minister, Department of Mines and Resources, Ottawa, to Canon H.G. Cook, Superintendent of ISA, MSCC, Ottawa.

12. NAC RG10 v.8801 f.651/25-13 pt.1, 6 August 1953, Rev. H.G. Cook, Superintendent of ISA, MSCC, Ottawa, to P.N. Phelan, Superintendent of Education, IAB, Ottawa.

13. NAC RG10 v.7185 f.1/25-1-7-5 pt.1, 10 November 1953, Rev. H.G. Cook, Superintendent of ISA, MSCC, Ottawa, to R.F. Davey, Acting Superintendent of Education, IAB, Ottawa.

14. NAC RG10 v.8753 f.601/25-1 pt.1, 2 March 1954, R.F. Davey, Acting Superintendent of Education, IAB, Ottawa, to J.T. Warden, Administrative Officer in Charge, IAB, Regina.

15. NAC RG10 v.8645 f.651/6-1 pt.1, 26 April 1954, J.T. Warden, Administrative Officer in Charge, IAB, Regina, to R.F. Davey, Acting Superintendent of Education, IAB, Ottawa.

16. NAC RG10 v.8645 f.651/6-1 pt.1, 11 May 1954, R.F. Davey, Acting Superintendent of Education, IAB, Ottawa, to Chief, Engineering and Construction Service, IAB, Ottawa.

17. NAC RG10 v.8645 f.651/6-1 pt.5, 13 July 1954, W.J. Hughes, Technical Officer, IAB, Regina, Report of Inspection of the Prince Albert Indian Residential School, Carlton Indian Agency, Saskatchewan.

18. NAC RG10 v.8754 f.651/25-1 pt.1, 27 October 1954, H.M. Jones, Director, IAB, Ottawa, to D. Knight, Chairman, Welfare Council of Greater Winnipeg.

19. NAC RG10 v.8754 f.651/25-1 pt.1, 19 July 1954, Rev. H.G. Cook, Superintendent of ISA, MSCC, Ottawa, to R.F. Davey, Superintendent of Education, IAB, Ottawa.

20. NAC RG10 v.8754 f.651/25-1 pt.1, 17 September 1954, H.M. Jones, Director, IAB,

Ottawa, to the Deputy Minister, Department of Citizenship and Immigration.

21. NAC RG10 v.8801 f.651/25-13 pt.1, Quarterly Per Capita Allowance Claim, Prince Albert Indian Residential School, for quarter ended 30 June 1955.

22. During the same period the Kamloops Indian Residential School had an authorized pupilage of 400 children and an actual attendance of 415 pupils. See NAC RG10 v.8795 f.1/25-13 pt.2, 17 April 1956, H.M. Jones, Director, IAB, Ottawa, to the Deputy Minister, Department of Citizenship and Immigration.

23. Ibid.

24. NAC RG10 v.6864 f.651/25-2 pt.3 and 4, Admissions and Discharges to the Prince Albert Indian Residential School, 1955–57.

25. Ibid. Occasionally there would be pupils at the school who were older than eighteen years.

26. While in theory Indian parents were seen as choosing to place their children in residential schools, in practice IAB personnel could also take the initiative in admitting children to these institutions. See Caldwell 1967:57.

27. NAC RG10 v.6864 f.651/25-2 pt.3 and 4, Admissions and Discharges to the Prince Albert Indian Residential School, 1955–57.

28. NAC RG10 v.8795 f.1/25-13 pt.2, 27 April 1956, R.F. Davey, Superintendent of Education, IAB, Ottawa, to R.F. Battle, Regional Supervisor of Indian Agencies, IAB, Calgary.

29. NAC RG10 v.8576 f.1/1-2-2-21 pt.1, 23 November 1956, Minutes of IAB Regional Inspectors' Conference, Ottawa.

30. Ibid.

31. See Miller 1996 for a discussion of this shift.

32. NAC RG10 v.8753 f.601/25-1 pt.1, 2 May 1957, H.B. Bodine, Regional Inspector of Indian Schools, IAB, Regina, to R.F. Davey, Superintendent of Education, IAB, Ottawa.

33. NAC RG10 v.8576 f.1/1-2-2-21, May 1958, Confidential Minutes of the Fourth Conference of Regional Inspectors of Indian Schools, IAB, Ottawa, April 10–11, 1958, and Minutes of Committee Meetings.

34. Ibid.

35. This increase in the number of Indian pupils represented not only an increase in population but also the impact of a more systematic enrolment of Indian children in educational programs.

36. ADSA, Box 55, Prince Albert Student Residence file, 28 October 1947, Bishop H.D. Martin, Prince Albert, to Rev. H.A. Calderwood, ISA, MSCC, Ottawa.

37. ADSA, Box 53, Indian School Administration file, 20 November 1952, Rev. H.G. Cook, ISA, MSCC, Ottawa, Memorandum entitled, "Indian Day Schools and Indian Residential Schools."

38. NAC RG10 v.8801 f.651/25-13 pt.1, 11 January 1957, R.F. Davey, Superintendent of Education, IAB, Ottawa, to E.S. Jones, Regional Supervisor of Indian Agencies, IAB, Regina.

39. NAC RG10 v.8801 f.651/25-13 pt.1, 30 January 1957, E.S. Jones, Regional Supervisor of Indian Agencies, IAB, Regina, to R.F. Davey, Superintendent of Education, IAB, Ottawa.

40. NAC RG10 v.8646 f.651/6-1 pt.11, 18 February 1960, H.M. Jones, Director, IAB, Ottawa, to the Deputy Minister of Citizenship and Immigration.

41. NAC RG10 v.8646 f.651/6-1 pt.9, 11 December 1957, Rev. H.G. Cook, Superin-

tendent of ISA, MSCC, Ottawa, to R.F. Davey, Superintendent of Education, IAB, Ottawa.

42. A past member of the 590 Air Cadet Squadron, Sol Sanderson, remembers it as the only all-Indian cadet squadron in Canada. He also recalls it being highly successful in Air Cadet competitions.

43. NAC RG10 v.8795 f.1/25-13 pt.6, 19 September 1959, Rev. W.E. Bramwell, Principal, PAIRS, to R.F. Davey, Superintendent of Education, IAB, Ottawa.

44. NAC RG10 v.7185 f.1/25-1-7-5 pt.1, 3 February 1960, Minutes of a Meeting of IAB Officials with Principals of Anglican Indian Residential Schools.

45. NAC RG10 v.8754 f.651/25-1, 19 July 1954, Rev. H.G. Cook, Superintendent of ISA, MSCC, Ottawa, to R.F. Davey, Superintendent of Education, IAB, Ottawa.

46. NAC RG10 v.7185 f.1/25-1-7-5 pt.1, 3 February 1960, Minutes of a Meeting of IAB Officials with Principals of Anglican Indian Residential Schools.

47. NAC RG10 v.8647 f.651/6-1 pt.11, 20 January 1960, Rev. H.G. Cook, Superintendent, ISA, MSCC, Ottawa, to R.F. Davey, Superintendent of Education, IAB, Ottawa.

48. NAC RG10 v.8647 f.651/6-1 pt.11, 23 March 1960, Rev. H.G. Cook, Superintendent, ISA, MSCC, Ottawa, to R.F. Davey, Superintendent of Education, IAB, Ottawa.

49. NAC RG10 v.8647 f.651/6-1 pt.11, 8 April 1960, R.F. Davey, Superintendent of Education, IAB, Ottawa, to Rev. H.G. Cook, Superintendent, ISA, MSCC, Ottawa.

50. NAC RG10 v.8647 f.651/6-1 pt.11, 5 November 1960, Rev. W.E. Bramwell, Principal, PAIRS, to R.F. Davey, Superintendent of Education, IAB, Ottawa.

51. NAC RG10 v.8648 f.651/6-1 pt.11, 18 February 1960, H.M. Jones, Director, IAB, Ottawa, to Deputy Minister, Department of Citizenship and Immigration.

52. Ibid.

53. NAC RG10 v.8647 f.651/6-1 pt.11, 13 February 1961, Education Committee, Prince Albert Chamber of Commerce, to Rev. Bramwell, Principal, PAIRS .

54. Civic finances in Prince Albert had been dealt a crushing and lasting blow in the early part of the century by an exorbitantly expensive and spectacularly unsuccessful hydro-electric development project known locally as the La Colle Falls "disaster." The accumulated civic debt was not paid off until 1965 and then only at the cost of foregoing many local amenities for more than fifty years. See Abrams 1966.

55. NAC RG10 v.8801 f.651/25-13, 22 May 1961, Rev. W.E. Bramwell, Principal, PAIRS, to Rev. Canon H.G. Cook, Superintendent of the ISA, MSCC, Ottawa.

56. Ibid.

57. NAC RG10 v.8753 f.601/25-1 pt.2, 25 April 1961, IAB, Ottawa, Draft of Policy Governing Placement of Indian Children in Boarding Home.

58. Ibid.

59. One of the former pupils of PAIRS who took part in the boarding home program in Prince Albert told me that this experience proved to be positive and beneficial.

60. NAC RG10 v.8647 f.651/6-1 pt.13, 21 June 1962, R.F. Davey, Chief, Education Division, IAB, Ottawa, to Chief, Engineering and Construction Division, IAB, Ottawa.

61. NAC RG10 v.8647 f.651/6-1 pt.13, 26 July 1962, Chief, Engineering and Construction Division, IAB, Ottawa, to R.F. Davey, Chief, Education Division, IAB, Ottawa.

62. NAC RG10 v.8647 f.651/6-1 pt.13, 5 July 1963, Canon A.H. Davis, General Secretary, MSCC, to Hon. Guy Favreau, Minister of Citizenship and Immigration.

63. NAC RG10 v.8647 f.651/6-1 pt.13, 17 October 1963, L.H. Wickwire, Chief,

Engineering and Construction Division, IAB, to Assistant Director, Education Division, IAB, Ottawa.

64. NAC RG10 v.8647 f.651/6-1 pt.13, 30 October 1963, P. Deziel, IAB, Ottawa, to Assistant Director, Education Division, IAB, Ottawa.

65. NAC RG10 v.8647 f.651/6-1 pt.14, 4 June 1964, G.J. Bowen, Assistant Chief, Construction and Engineering Division, IAB, Ottawa, to R.F. Davey, Assistant Director of Education, IAB, Ottawa.

66. NAC RG10 v.8647 f.651/6-1 pt.13, 1 May 1964, R.F. Battle, Director, IAB, Ottawa, to J.W. Oliver, City Commissioner, Prince Albert.

67. NAC RG10 v.8647 f.651/6-1 pt.14, 4 August 1964, Chief, Engineering and Construction Division, IAB, Ottawa, to Assistant Director of Education, IAB, Ottawa.

68. NAC RG10 v.8647 f.651/6-1 pt.14, 9 December 1964, Rev. W.E. Bramwell, Principal, PAIRS, to Rev. Canon T. Jones, Director, Residential Schools and Hostels Division, MSCC, Toronto.

69. NAC RG10 v.8647 f.651/6-1 pt.14, 10 December 1964, R.H. Gent, District School Superintendent, IAB, Prince Albert, to Director, Educational Services, IAB, Ottawa.

70. Ibid.

71. Caldwell 1967:108. Note that PAIRS, along with all other schools included in the study, employed the use of corporal punishment under the control of school principals.

72. While individual bishops opposed the transfer of control of residential schools to the federal government, other elements of the Anglican Church had by 1969 begun to promote a critical evaluation of the church's relationship with Aboriginal peoples. See, for instance, Hendry 1969.

73. ADSA, Box 53, Indian School Administration file, 20 February 1969, Bishop of Saskatchewan, Prince Albert, to J.G. Diefenbaker, M.P., House of Commons, Ottawa.

74. ADSA, Box 53, Indian School Administration file, 26 February 1969, Jean Chretien, Minister of Indian and Northern Affairs, Ottawa, to Bishop J.A. Watton, Schumacher, Ontario.

75. ADSA, Box 53, Indian Affairs file, 16 September 1969, Bishop Crump, Prince Albert, to F.A. Clarke, Regional Director, DIAND, Regina.

Chapter 5

After the White Paper

The Prince Albert Student Residence[1]

The year 1969 marked a watershed in Canadian Indian administration and in the history of Indian residential schooling in Prince Albert. In June 1969 the federal government unveiled a set of policy proposals in a White Paper designed to eliminate within a period of five years the special legal and constitutional status of Canada's Indians and facilitate the abolition of both the Indian Act and the Department of Indian Affairs within a five-week period.[2] Indians were to be granted title and control of reserve lands and would thereafter receive services from and pay taxes to provincial and municipal governments. Federal funding allocated to Indian administration would initially be transferred to the provinces, although this subsidy would be phased out. Other proposals included creation of a $50 million economic development fund and the appointment of an Indian claims commissioner.

The White Paper proposed a genuinely radical "solution" to the "Indian problem" by simply abolishing federal Indian administration. After a century of coercive tutelage and legislated paternalism, which had intentionally segregated Indians from the rest of Canadian society and subjected Aboriginal children and families to programs of assimilation, the federal government now intended to transform Indians into ordinary Canadians by simply redefining them as ordinary Canadians and withdrawing the laws and administrative practices that had long governed virtually every aspect of their lives. Having systematically restricted Aboriginal peoples' ability to develop and pursue their own livelihoods and control their lands and resources as they saw fit, the federal government would suddenly expect Indians to resolve or endure the growing political, social and economic inequalities that separated them from non-Aboriginal Canadians after a century of federal Indian administration. Whatever the rhetoric used to promote the White Paper, the fact remained that Indians would be arbitrarily thrust into a set of circumstances not of their own making. Once again, federal officials had determined what was "in the best interests of Indians" without even bothering to engage in meaningful consultation with the people whose lives were to be so fundamentally affected.[3]

The officials who drafted the White Paper seriously misjudged the sentiments of reserve communities and the capability of Indian representatives. Indian associations throughout the length and breadth of Canada denounced the White Paper in the strongest terms, interpreting its proposals as advocating a form of cultural genocide. In June 1970 Prime Minister Trudeau backed down from the position outlined in the White Paper and promised that his government would not implement proposals unacceptable to Indian people. In the course of the White Paper controversy provincial, territorial and national Indian associations emerged to serve as articulate and determined representatives of Indian people. As well as forcing the federal government to retreat from its ill-considered proposals, Indian associations such as the Federation of Saskatchewan Indians (FSI) championed the right of Indians to determine their own destiny. Significantly, a number of the young leaders of the FSI were themselves graduates of the Prince Albert Indian Residential School.

The restructuring and renaming of PAIRS that took place in 1969 reflected both the "integrationist" values that underpinned the White Paper proposals and a federal labour ruling that obliged all non-teaching staff at residential schools to become federal employees. The latter measure effectively eliminated any further basis for direct participation by denominational employees in Indian residential schooling. Indeed, in the wake of the Caldwell Report, residential schools across Canada began to terminate operations as federal officials opted to replace the educational services that schools had previously provided through joint tuition agreements with provincial and local educational authorities. In Prince Albert the implementation of joint schooling arrangements had, by 1969, already proceeded to the point that PAIRS was serving as a residential facility rather than a residential school. This transformation was acknowledged in the decision to rename it the Prince Albert Student Residence (PASR) when federal officials took control of the facility from the Anglican Church. Nonetheless, some strands of the longstanding working relationship in Prince Albert between church and state were maintained. The administrator placed in charge of PASR may have been a federal civil servant, but he was also an Anglican lay reader and an active member of the Executive Committee of Synod for the Diocese of Saskatchewan.[4]

The Limitations of Integrated Schooling

Notwithstanding this structural alteration in the administration of the facility, many of the everyday operations of PASR continued much as before. Each day Indian children were transported from the residence to one of the many public or Roman Catholic Separate Schools in Prince Albert that had contracted with the federal government to provide schooling for Indian students. Care was taken to ensure that in no school did Indian children represent more than 50 percent of the student body. Indian children were viewed as portable individuals who could be distributed to any one of a number of schools at the pleasure of local school board officials. Nor could Indian children assume that they would continue and complete their elementary schooling in any one school. In consequence, decisions concerning which schools Indian children would be assigned to were made not on the basis of student-centred objectives such as keeping brothers and sisters together in the same school, but according to bureaucratic guidelines and contractual agreements. The logistical demands of merely busing the children to and from these various schools each day were quite staggering.

The experience of Indian children in attending these schools is not examined in detail in this report for the reasons outlined in the Introduction. Nonetheless, individuals employed at the residence during these years indicate that one of the most difficult aspects of their work was to witness Indian children breaking into tears on many mornings when they were dropped off in front of their designated schools. Within the city schools a substantial proportion of Indian children were assigned to special education classes, an arrangement that some observers viewed as being tantamount to establishing informal educational ghettoes in spite of the so-called "integrated" schooling agreements. Although Indian children constituted a minority within each school, they frequently represented a majority of the students enrolled in special education classes. The suspicion was that an unduly large proportion of Indian children were being labelled as lacking the academic ability to perform satisfactorily and, thus, were frequently placed in groups where less was expected of them and less time and attention was given to them by teachers.

The long-term contractual agreements entered into by the federal government with the Prince Albert Public and Separate School Boards[5] provided the city schools with dependable and lucrative annual tuition payments based on the number of Indian children assigned to schools at the beginning of September rather than the number still remaining at the end of the school year. Additional capital grants provided by the federal government to the schools permitted the construction of gymnasia and specialized facilities such as chemistry and physics laboratories that served the needs of those students—non-Indian as well as Indian—enrolled in the academic stream. While these and other financial inducements were supposed to purchase high calibre educational services for Indian children, it is not apparent that federal authorities took any special effort to monitor the social, emotional and educational treatment extended to Indian children. Conditions within these schools seem to have been simply deemed by Indian Affairs officials to be acceptable or, at least, the best that could be done under the circumstances.

This raises the question of the extent to which federal officials' hands were or were not tied by jurisdictional boundaries. Since education has always been constitutionally a provincial responsibility and since the churches had traditionally subcontracted to provide the delivery of schooling on behalf of the Department of Indian Affairs, the federal government did not possess extensive in-house expertise in the educational field. This, it might be argued, placed DIAND officials in the position of having to respect and defer to provincial and local school authorities on matters concerning the quality of education provided to Indian children in joint schools. Yet notwithstanding these jurisdictional and professional considerations, federal officials who negotiated and were supposed to monitor the joint schooling programs funded on behalf of Indian children surely should have been capable of exercising at least a basic level of attentiveness and interest in the ways in which Aboriginal children were treated.

From the perspective of some Indian observers, however, those city teachers who were openly identified as having mistreated Indian children usually had little to fear from federal officials. DIAND restricted its involvement in Indian education in Prince Albert to negotiating expensive contracts and then ensuring that Indian children were delivered to the schools. Given this approach, it is scarcely surprising that many Indian parents and leaders suspected that DIAND was paying a great deal more for Indian education than the value their children were receiving.

Although since the nineteenth century Indian parents and leaders had repeatedly demonstrated concern regarding the forms and conditions of schooling provided for their children both in Prince Albert and elsewhere, Canadian Indian administration had traditionally operated on the assumption that Indians did not know what was in their best interests and, thus, needed to be subjected to bureaucratic tutelage. This ostensibly well-meaning program of administration actually comprised a system of coercion that sought to strip Indians of their languages and cultures and force their assimilation into Canadian society. Indian communities had resisted these assumptions and objectives from the outset but, for many decades, had not been in a position from which they might realistically have challenged the arbitrary exercise of power by federal officials. In the years following the White Paper controversy, Indians' political demands were heard widely in Canada for virtually the first time. Yet in seeking to reconstruct their relationship with governments along more positive lines, Indian bands and associations confronted a plethora of official understandings, institutions, arrangements and practices that badly needed to be addressed and refashioned.

The Call for Indian Control of Indian Education

The 1972 presentation by the National Indian Brotherhood[6] of a policy calling for Indian control of Indian education reflected the abiding interest of Indian parents and leaders in this vital field. From this point on, the struggle to reform Indian education would feature successive initiatives by Aboriginal people to exercise greater control over curricular matters and the allocation of educational resources earmarked for Indian children. One of the first initiatives began in 1973 when the Prince Albert District Chiefs (PADC), with assistance from the FSI, undertook to intervene in the direction of the Prince Albert Student

Residence. Three preliminary steps marked the beginning of a process to establish Indian control of Indian education in Prince Albert that would take twelve years to complete.

Central to this process was the creation of an Indian Board of Directors for PASR (the members of which were to be appointed by band chiefs and councils in the Prince Albert district) that would work with DIAND to oversee the operations of the residence. According to one of the Indian leaders involved, church and government officials opposed this step with whatever resources they could muster.[7] Church leaders attempted to rally leading Indian members of the Anglican Church against the changes, and federal officials sought to employ whatever influence they had with Indian School Committees towards the same end. However, attempts to divide First Nations people were not successful, so the new management structure was implemented. The federal government maintained financial and operational control over the residence and continued to serve as the employer for child care, maintenance and other staff employed at PASR. The new arrangement did, however, permit an Indian to be placed in the senior administrative position at the institution for the first time in the long history of Indian residential schooling in Prince Albert.[8] While this was a long overdue step in the desired direction, it still comprised a good deal less than actual Indian control of Indian education.

The agreements federal officials had signed with local school authorities left little room for immediate transformation, but members of the new board of directors were determined to take every opportunity to pursue the overall task of reshaping the objectives and structure of educational services for Indian children in Prince Albert. As well as registering dissatisfaction with many previously unquestioned aspects of the joint schooling arrangements, the board insisted upon the resumption of on-site schooling for elementary students at the residence. DIAND officials reluctantly accepted this demand and authorized the construction of a temporary school block in the form of a number of portable trailers in 1974. This new school, which initially offered grades one to three, was to operate as an Indian-directed institution within a larger federal facility. Teachers and associate teachers at the new school were formally employed by the Wahpeton Band on behalf of the PADC.[9] In subsequent years more grades were taught at the residence in basement rooms in some of the cottages. The curriculum adopted at the residence school followed provincial guidelines but also featured Cree language instruction and other cultural components. The use of Indian associate teachers and cultural presentations by elders such as Angus Mirasty became significant aspects of the program at what was one of Saskatchewan's first schools to be substantially directed by Indians.

Prior to 1985 several approaches were tested in the federally-controlled residential component of PASR. In an attempt to create the "homey" atmosphere originally envisioned by those who re-designed the facility in the 1960s, child care workers were encouraged to have their families live with them in the cottages. An attempt was also made to locate all siblings within the same cottage. Some of these arrangements proved satisfactory while others did not. For instance, the presence of staff members' families on campus allowed the non-Indian husband of one of the non-Indian child care workers then employed by DIAND to molest a number of Indian girls between 1976 and 1983, a situation that was not revealed until the 1990s when George Albert Zimmerman was charged and convicted of a dozen sex-related offences.[10] On the other hand, Indian employees at PASR led the way in encouraging students to maintain closer contact with their families by allowing them to telephone home on a weekly basis and urging them to write regularly to their parents. Moreover, instead of merely mailing children's academic progress reports to parents, the school adopted the practice of having a representative of the residence take report cards (along with plainly and understandably written reports on each child's general behaviour and social development) to reserve communities where these could be presented and explained to parents.

The importance of monitoring behaviour and taking a proactive approach to facilitate the social development of children sent to PASR increased each year. Throughout this period, the proportion of children sent to Prince Albert due to a lack of educational facilities in their home communities steadily decreased while the proportion assigned for social or behavioural reasons rose. An evaluation of PASR's child care program conducted in 1977 provided insight into the changing nature of the student population from the perspective of the child care workers:

> There is general agreement that more children are coming to the Residence with behavior problems. Often the children report alcoholism in the family or come from broken homes. Most of the CCWs [child care workers] thought there will need to be fewer children per dorm or more staff if the pattern of children with behavior problems continues. Many staff members said that they cannot get all the work done if they have several such children in their dorms. "You just can't tell those children what to do and expect them to go ahead." "I just don't have time to counsel—I start to talk with somebody and there is always someone else needing something."[11]

The report also noted that vandalism had become a problem at the residence and suggested that the provision of closer supervision and additional funding for an enhanced recreational program would help to overcome a situation where some children were being left too much to their own devices and, thus, were frequently getting into trouble.

While the child care workers understood the role of PASR as offering a service to parents who for whatever reason were unable to take care of their children themselves, they felt that children who were admitted with serious emotional or social problems and required one-to-one or professional care ought not to be accepted into the residence under the existing staffing conditions. There was also dissatisfaction with the screening process, and it was noted that some children were being sent to PASR without sufficient consideration being given to the lack of resources at the institution to serve their special needs. The desirability of providing on-site training for the child care workers in counselling and group work was one of the report's key recommendations.

Moving Towards a Transfer of Responsibilities

By the late 1970s it was anticipated that the federal government would eventually transfer operation of the Indian student residences in Saskatchewan to bands or district chiefs' organizations.[12] In the meantime, DIAND performed an ambiguous role in managing student residences, continuing to fund the residences and to serve as the employer of all non-educational employees at PASR. Initially, when the district offices of DIAND had many more personnel and managed a broader range of departmental activities, it was possible for the PASR board of directors and administrator to deal directly with district office managers on matters pertaining to the residence. By the 1980s, however, the drive to reduce and centralize the operations of DIAND resulted in much smaller district offices that fulfilled more of an accounting than a managerial or decision-making function. In consequence, it became steadily more difficult for residence personnel to attract the interest and attention of DIAND to address operational issues at PASR and other residences.

There was also a perception among those who were actively involved in the running of PASR during the 1970s and early 1980s that departmental officials were inclined to be more readily responsive to the interests of the Prince Albert school boards than to those of the Indian-directed school operating at the residence. It was felt that the principals of public or separate schools encountered much less difficulty than their counterpart at the residence school in having individual Indian students classified as special needs students, who would then bring a higher level of institutional funding from DIAND. Departmental officials were also perceived as engaging in a "divide and conquer" strategy in dealing with the province's student residences, a view that in 1982 prompted the creation of the Coalition of Saskatchewan Indian Student Residences. As the largest student residence in Saskatchewan, PASR and its successor institution played a key part in an ongoing effort to foster unity and co-operation between these evolving Indian educational and child care institutions.

Another area of concern for staff involved informal relations between PASR and its children and the city and people of Prince Albert. Notwithstanding the fact that Indian residential schooling had made substantial contributions to the economy of Prince Albert both directly and indirectly for the better part of a century, city officials seemed to take for granted the advantages of having such an institution in their jurisdiction. Since the gymnasium at the residence was the largest auditorium in the city, for many years it was utilized for high school graduation ceremonies staged by city schools and for a variety of other purposes by non-Indian groups. A swimming pool constructed at the residence site when it was a military base was the only such facility in Prince Albert for many years and was popular with city residents and much appreciated during the summer months, a time when Indian students were typically returned to their home reserves.[13] Yet when residence staff repeatedly requested that the City install a traffic light at the intersection of 22nd Street West and 6th Avenue so that children from the residence could cross the road safely on their way to and from school they encountered resistance from city officials. Only after mounting a detailed study of the pedestrian and vehicular traffic in this particular intersection on weekdays, and incidentally demonstrating that a substantial number of the children endangered by crossing this intersection happened to be non-Indians, were residence personnel able to change minds at City Hall.

A longstanding inclination on the part of residents of Prince Albert to blame the Indian children for anonymous and imagined misdeeds, over and above any actual mischief for which they may have been responsible, was dramatically escalated when the Peter Ballantyne Band proposed in the late 1970s to select the residence site under the Treaty Lands Entitlement program and transform it into an Indian reserve. This measure, which would exempt Indian employees of PASR from paying income tax on their earnings, was endorsed by the Prince Albert District Chiefs in 1978 in the face of much apprehension, rumour-mongering and outright opposition on the part of some city residents. Nevertheless, a Privy Council order adopted four years later established the site as the Opawakoscikan Reserve and designated it to be used for educational purposes under Section 18(2) of the Indian Act as long as it might be required by the PADC.

In 1980 the creation of an education board by the PADC to replace the seven-year-old governing structure erected to oversee the initiation of Indian-directed educational operations at PASR represented another important step in the evolution of the institution. By establishing a specialized education board the PADC enhanced its capacity to grasp the complex issues and procedures involved in retaining and transforming the residence both for educational and social development purposes. The subsequent evolution of the PADC into the Prince Albert District Chiefs' Council (PADCC) and later the Prince Albert Tribal Council (PATC) prepared the way for its twelve member bands to develop a more systematic and professional basis for administering programs on its own behalf as well as for individual member bands that might seek its services in implementing and managing particular programs. Thus, it was due to the sustained efforts of the PATC education board that, in 1984, the residence school was allowed to expand beyond the confines of what was then the ten-year-old "temporary" school block by renting half of the nearby Queen Elizabeth School.[14] This permitted the residence-based school to move beyond the grade five level.

Aside from this extension, throughout the early 1980s the impending transfer of the entire residence operation to the PADC led DIAND to minimize its expenditures on the institution. Beginning in 1980 DIAND employees hired at the residence were employed on a temporary basis with few of the normal employee benefits. After several years of PADC lobbying, the department agreed to reclassify temporary staff members in somewhat more attractive terms, but there remained a strong sense among employees that the entire residence operation was being kept at an artificially low level. Demand for admissions to PASR remained high because the number of children whose needs could not be satisfactorily met in their home communities continued to climb. Despite employee efforts to increase staffing and to obtain training that would better equip them to meet the special requirements of a growing proportion of the residence population, PASR was essentially forced to make do with inadequate resources. It carried on nonetheless, performing its officially unacknowledged but important task of acting as an institutional safety net that kept many Indian boys and girls from being permanently removed from their communities, placed in care and assigned to foster homes or provincial group home facilities, or even put up for adoption out of the province or out of the country. Whatever its shortcomings, the school and residential facility operated at PASR continued to serve this vital need, the importance of which was well understood and steadfastly defended by education board members.

Notes

1. Access to pertinent federal government documents from this period could not be arranged. I have, however, had an opportunity to discuss the developments and events of this period with a number of individuals who played key roles at that time, including Howard Bighead, Larry Goldade, Cliff Star and Sol Sanderson. I wish to express my appreciation for their generosity in discussing these matters with me.
2. For further detail on the 1969 White Paper and the controversy it sparked, see Dyck 1991:108–12.
3. See Weaver 1981 for a full account of the drafting of the White Paper after federal officials staged a set of less than sincere consultations with Aboriginal peoples.
4. See Payton 1974:162. Sol Sanderson, the Chief of James Smith Band and the vice-president in charge of education for the FSI at that time, recalls that the Diocese of Saskatchewan, along with other denominational agencies that had previously operated Indian residential schools in the province, continued to have a financial stake in the operation of the student residences. Apparently the denominations continued to receive some funding in conjunction with student residences until approximately 1973.
5. Some of these contracts, which ran for up to twenty-five years, are only now coming to an end.
6. The National Indian Brotherhood was transformed into the Assembly of First Nations in the early 1980s.
7. Sol Sanderson provided this information.
8. In 1973 Jim Roberts was appointed the first Indian administrator of PASR and

Howard Bighead was appointed the first Indian head child care worker. Bighead was appointed acting head of the residence in 1975 and was confirmed in the administrator's position in 1976.

9. The provision of busing services for PASR was also transferred to the Wahpeton Band.
10. For newspaper reports of the court proceedings in the Zimmerman case see the Prince Albert *Daily Herald,* November 15–22, 1994.
11. PAISEC f.140, Box B, November 1977, Child Care Workers Evaluation, Planning and Research, DIAND, 672/1-18.
12. These district chiefs' organizations subsequently evolved into tribal councils.
13. An expensive and not terribly successful solar heating project was funded by the federal government to heat the swimming pool. In due course the solar heating equipment was removed and the aging swimming pool filled in by the federal government.
14. The neighbourhood around this school had matured demographically, thereby leaving vacant classrooms that the school board was willing to rent.

Chapter 6

Realizing a Vision
The Prince Albert Indian
Student Education Centre[1]

The Department of Indian and Northern Affairs' (INAC) transfer and consolidation of the Prince Albert Student Residence (PASR) with the residence school program under the direction of the Prince Albert District Chiefs Council (PADCC) in May 1985 constituted a key turning point in the lengthy history of Indian residential schooling in that city. Before delving into the details of this arrangement and the subsequent operations of the institution, however, it is necessary to identify some of the underlying issues and interests involved in this transaction.

To begin with, although the term "program transfer" may have seemed to federal officials to describe what took place in Prince Albert in 1985, this transaction, when viewed in a historical perspective, comprised much more than a mere administrative shuffling or reassignment of responsibilities. In one sense this development marked the culmination of the political process initiated in 1973 when leaders from the Prince Albert district had insisted upon the right of Indians to be involved in directing an institution that figured so significantly in the lives of their children. Looking back even further in time, the takeover of PASR by the PADCC represented a victory for patient determination on the part of Indian parents and leaders, past and present, to overcome all obstacles placed in their way since the negotiation of Treaty Six and, thereby, to ensure that their children would be provided with appropriate educational services. The potential value of formal schooling had been apparent to Indian parents since the arrival of James Nisbet in the 1860s. Moreover, Chief James Smith and other leaders had been prominent supporters of Emmanuel College when it became an Indian boarding school in the early 1890s.

What Indian parents wanted for their children in the nineteenth century and in the 1980s was an education that would equip them with the knowledge and skills required to participate as freely and effectively as they choose in the new society that emerged in Western Canada. What they received from church and state were often well-meaning but ultimately demeaning forms of schooling based on the premise that Indians did not know what was in their best interests. Underlying most denominational and government educational programs for Indians in Saskatchewan and elsewhere was a firm belief that Aboriginal cultures and modes of social organization were "primitive" and "inferior" to those of Euro-Canadians. This racist belief had, of course, provided the justification for appropriating Aboriginal lands across Canada. In the classroom this discriminatory approach led to a displacement of purposes: instead of focusing upon what Indian parents wanted their children to learn, teachers were diverted to tasks of moral and cultural engineering. In short, schools were expected to strip Indians of their languages, cultures and identities. What Indian children were supposed to learn in school was that they were not acceptable as they were and that they must strive to become unlike their parents.

In hindsight, what is remarkable is that so many Indian parents and leaders did not turn their backs entirely on schooling, even though over the years an increasing number had personal experience of what their children were likely to encounter in either residential or day schools. Parents and leaders did attempt to keep an eye on conditions in schools and, on many occasions complained about the mistreatment of their children despite being regularly discouraged from visiting these institutions. They were also concerned about the frequently poor quality of instruction provided to Indian pupils due to the systematic underfunding of Indian education by the federal government. Yet on both counts their concerns tended to be discounted or dismissed precisely because the belief structure of federal Indian administration and its associated educational system functioned on the assumption that Indian parents were probably unable to comprehend what was required to educate their children properly.

The problem was not that all or even most government or denominational personnel associated with the operation of Indian schools intentionally set out to harm Indian pupils or prevent them from obtaining a good education. Nor were the individuals employed in these schools invariably lacking in compassion or commitment. There was, indeed, evidence that many teachers and other school personnel believed that what they were doing would be in the best interests of Indian children in the long run. But, to paraphrase a proverb, "the road to Hell is paved with good intentions." Notwithstanding the conscientious efforts of some individual teachers and bureaucrats, the inescapable shortcomings of the Indian education system resulted from the basic principles upon which it was founded and the manner in which these deprecated and disempowered Indian people, young and old. The environment that resulted tolerated or shielded the culturally condescending, reprehensible and even abusive behaviour of some staff members.

In taking over responsibility for directing PAISEC the people of the PADCC, through their elected political representatives, were finally enabled to shape the overall manner in which Indian children who required residential schooling would be treated in the Prince Albert facility. But it was not as though they were starting with a blank slate. By 1985 the field of Indian education was littered with the prejudices, practices and products of more than a century of residential schooling by church and state. The growing incidence of social and behavioural problems that afflicted so many of the children sent to Prince Albert was itself part of the legacy of the coercive tutelage that had traditionally guided Indian administration and residential schooling. Accordingly, one of the first and most difficult tasks facing the new institution was to recognize how deeply ingrained within it were the submerged and often assumed working assumptions about how a residential educational facility for Indians should be operated. In effect, a substantial amount of "unlearning" would have to be completed by all concerned before the new institution could establish more responsive and respectful ways of tending to the social and educational needs of Indian children. To signal just how fundamental a break with the past this new institution intended to make, the leaders of the PADCC gave it a new name: the Prince Albert Indian Student Education centre (PAISEC).

Charting a New Direction

Formidable challenges confronted PADCC leaders in charting a new direction for PAISEC. They had to demonstrate that PAISEC would not be merely a new name for what amounted to another version of an archaic and discredited institutional form, the Indian residential school. As well as making PAISEC fully accepting of Aboriginal cultures and accountable to parents, band leaders and the PADCC Education Board, it was important to demonstrate that it would not be organized primarily to suit the convenience of the personnel who worked within it but to be responsive to the needs of the children whom it served. Since INAC's past experience of managing residential schools and student residences offered little in the way of a model for enhancing PAISEC's operations, a good deal of initiative, sensitivity and courage would be required to discover appropriate ways of realizing the ambitious objectives set for the new centre. High standards of professionalism would have to be established and maintained by PAISEC staff. Moreover, given that PAISEC was not simply an Indian-controlled school but one that also cared for its children twenty-four hours a day, it could not simply compare itself to other band schools. PAISEC would, in many respects, become a unique facility that offered highly specialized and much needed services to Indian children who would otherwise be forced to leave their communities and enter into care under the jurisdiction of the provincial government.[2] Children such as these were frequently lost to their families and communities on a permanent basis, and it was this pattern that PAISEC was instructed to bring to an end.

    INAC took control of an institution that had been systematically underfunded by federal officials for many years in anticipation of its eventual transfer to the PADCC. From the bureaucratic perspective, the transfer offered an opportunity to off-load upon Indians a maximum of responsibilities and a minimum of budgetary resources.[3] What was more, as soon as they had passed over to PAISEC the task of providing institutional care for rising numbers of children who required much more than simply classroom instruction, INAC officials began to define and treat PAISEC as though it was simply an ordinary school providing routine educational services and residential accommodation.

What this amounted to was an instrumental denial by federal officials of the manner in which residential schooling in Prince Albert, as elsewhere, had long been used informally by government to address the need for child and family services upon Indian reserves. Sending orphans and children with social and behavioural problems to residential schools had been an inexpensive way of covering the relative lack of reserve social services provided by the department. Providing appropriate care for these children tended to require more of the staff's time and expertise than was the case for other students, but additional resources were not granted for this purpose. Instead, residential school employees were left to get on with jobs that became more demanding and less attractive year by year. The strain this placed on staff members did nothing to improve the quality of life for either them or the children placed under their charge. The Caldwell Report (1967) had called for the government to end its traditional exploitation of underpaid and overworked denominational employees. Church involvement in the operation of PASR may have largely ended in 1969, but systematic underfunding and understaffing of the institution persisted and even worsened in the 1970s and early 1980s.

By 1985 the demands made upon PAISEC staff members to address children's social and behavioural problems were vastly greater than had been the case even eighteen years earlier, yet INAC stubbornly chose to view and to fund PAISEC as though it was just another school unless and until it was forced to do otherwise. Even then such acknowledgements by federal officials were carefully limited and kept on a temporary basis. INAC's strategy of denial would make the operation of PAISEC far more difficult than necessary. The objectives the PADCC set for PAISEC did not readily conform with the bureaucratic categories and projections of the federal government. In fact, by the 1980s INAC had managed to close almost all former residential schools across Canada. Only in Saskatchewan had Indian people demanded the right to take over and completely transform these institutions so that they would serve the needs of Indian communities as defined by these communities. The struggle waged in the face of continued resistance on the part of federal officials by the people and leaders of the PADCC to build and defend their own vision of what PAISEC could become and what services it ought to provide meant that the creation of this new institution comprised an essential exercise in the realization of Indian government and self-determination.

A year before the creation of PAISEC the management board of the PADCC granted permission to the administration of the residence to proceed with a study of the existing child care program at the institution.[4] The objectives of the study were to review the placement and admission process, assess the child care program and make recommendations for improving operational procedures. Research for the study was conducted primarily between January and April, 1985, and the final report was completed and submitted in November of that year. This study provided insight into the operations of the institution just prior to the PADCC takeover and during the first few months of PAISEC's operations.

The study confirmed the perceptions and experience of PASR staff concerning the changing composition of the student population at the residence. In 1969 there had been approximately as many children attending PASR for educational[5] as for social reasons;[6] by the early 1980s socially-related admissions accounted for 77 percent of the students. In the fall of 1985, students aged six to ten years represented 36.7 percent of the student population, those aged eleven to fourteen made up over half (52.4 percent) and children aged fifteen years and older accounted for the final 10.9 percent of admissions. Eight of the twelve Prince Albert district bands had children placed at the residence; Lac la Ronge and Peter Ballantyne bands together placed 81.6 percent of all students attending PAISEC. Some 40 percent of students were attending the institution for their first year, 40 percent for their second to fourth year and 20 percent for their fifth or more year.

A survey conducted among Prince Albert students as part of the larger study indicated that, although a majority of the students at the residence (66 percent) identified education as being their main reason for being at the residence, approximately the same proportion (61 percent) reported that socially-related factors had predominated in the explanations provided to them by their parents or guardians concerning why they had been sent there. The majority of students interviewed agreed with their parents' decision, but approximately 26 percent thought they should not have been sent to Prince Albert. Similarly, a majority of students reported being satisfied with their experience at the residence while a third were clearly dissatisfied or ambivalent. When specifically asked what they liked about the residence, students frequently mentioned aspects of the sports and recreation and child care programs along with other school activities:

"all the new friends I made, meals, feeling of security and that the people who work here really care."

"I can sleep good at night, no one bothers me, I get up in time for school too."

"I got to meet more people, opportunity to go to school regularly, . . . security the Residence has to offer. I feel safe."

"I like playing soccer, all kinds of sports, they don't do those things on the reserve."[7]

Some students did not the regulations and discipline imposed, the unruly behaviour of some other students and the lack of recreational opportunities for girls:

"I don't like going outside, I don't like the fighting and name calling."

"I don't like getting a spanking, going to bed early and cauliflower."

"I don't like being here at the Residence and going to foster homes and then back again . . . it would be nice to stay with my sister."

"Some students are bothersome because they don't like Dene students and I don't have any relatives here."[8]

Students' suggestions for improving and changing the residence included the provision of more social and recreational activities, greater flexibility in the management of discipline, and also greater control over abusive behaviour on the part of other students. A parallel survey of parents indicated that 88 percent of those interviewed anticipated applying to have their children placed in PAISEC in subsequent years.[9]

Child care workers at the residence viewed their primary responsibility as that of substitute parent for children, although approximately half of them also saw it as part of their job to contribute to the children's educational development. The vast majority (83 percent) of child care workers were frustrated with the lack of social, educational, family and medical information made available to them from reserve communities when children were admitted to the residence.[10] From the perspective of these staff members, improvement in their contact and communication with parents was badly needed. The nurturing of these links would enhance their ability to support the development of the children under their care. Toward this end, child care workers called for one or two visits by staff members to home communities each year.

They also advocated halving the ratio of children to child care workers from the then existing level of twenty-four to one. This would permit the offering of a broader range of social and recreational activities, which would, it was believed, serve to ease some of the difficulties with students' behaviour. In the opinion of most child care workers, a more thorough screening process prior to admission would prevent children with very serious behavioural problems from being sent to the residence. The insufficient staff resources did not permit intensive individual attention to extremely "high need" students.

𝔄 𝔇ay in the 𝔏ife of a 𝔈hild 𝔈are 𝔚orker
The nature and scope of the demands made upon PAISEC staff members is illustrated by a set of diary entries recorded by child care workers, which outline

their daily round of activities. The following entry for a weekday in January 1985 was submitted to the research team by one child care worker who supervised twenty-four girls, ranging from six to sixteen years of age:

6.45 am	Made the little girl lunch who [was going] to La Ronge for a funeral. She also had $8.75 for her canteen.
7.00 am	Wake up the girls to wash, brush their hair, fix their beds while breakfast is being prepared.
7.30–7.50 am	Breakfast, say Grace.
7.50 am	Brush their teeth.
8.00 am	Medication given. Each girl to do their daily duties.
8.15 am	Had a talk to two girls that joined Al-a-teen as the past two Mondays they've had an excuse to miss [meetings]. I told them this program would be good for them as they talked about an alcohol problem at home.
	Tea towels to wash downstairs, also underclothes and socks.
8.20 am	Get a girl ready for her doctor's appointment, at 8.30 to be at the infirmary. Also check their work or chores.
	Kitchen girls to do their floors yet.
8.25 am	Check the rooms to see if they're clean and tidy.
8.30 am	Two girls ready to get on their bus at 8.40 am.
8.35 am	Get more girls ready for school, the ones that walk make sure they all have their winter outer wear on. Make sure they have their homework. Glasses, etc.
8.45 am	The remainder of the girls that attend school here at the Residence brush their hair and get ready for school a repeat of the 8.35 am duty.

8.55 am	Make sure all lights are out.
9.00 am	Got a girl ready to go home for a funeral. Phone the school that a girl has gone to her doctor's appointment.
9.05–10.30 am	Child Care Workers' Meeting in the Board Room
10.30–11.45 am	[Time Off]
11.45 am	Girls come in for lunch, they wash, pour juice and eat for 20 minutes.
12.15 pm	Girls clean the dining room and kitchen. Brush their teeth.
12.20 pm	Medication given out.
12.25 pm	Two girls to get ready for their school bus. They also need skates for this afternoon.
12.30 pm	Some girls brush their hair and get ready for school the ones that have to walk—a ten to fifteen minute walk.
	The rest brush their hair and get ready for school. They go to school here at the residence.
12.45–3.30 pm	[Time] Off.
3.30 pm	Girls start coming home. Nurse phoned from the infirmary—would like a girl to go over as soon as she comes in.
3.45 pm	Get the girls seated for homework.
	Study period. If they're not done, they sit down again after supper.
4.30 pm	Pick up medication and check the doctor's list at the office. Three girls haven't arrived back to the dorm yet from school.

4.40 pm	Checked the laundry box at the laundry room for missing laundry—nothing there so went to check the sewing room in the discard book—the items were discarded.
4.55 pm	The girls go to wash and brush up for supper and line up [to] go over to the dining room.
5.00 pm	[Time] Off.
5.30 pm	Girls brush their teeth.
5.40 pm	Girls do their chores.
5.45 pm	A girl was picked up to go and visit her mom who is in town for two days or so, they'll be at the Marlboro [Hotel].
6.00 pm	Medication given.
6.00–7.00 pm	Free time for all. Too cold to go out, so they play with the games the dorm has, some have visitors.
	A girl made a cake for a little girl who is having her seventh birthday. She got a letter today which was read to her. She also had ten dollars in it. Her sister also got a letter and ten dollars.
7.00 pm	Games down in the playroom for the party.
8.00 pm	They wash up, hand in their under clothes and socks.
8.15 pm	Birthday cake and hot chocolate for night lunch. Shoes out by their doors, in case of fire.
8.30 pm	First group 6–9 years. Bed time.
8.45 pm	Have a couple of girls wash cups. The girls that work in the dining room set table for breakfast.
9.00 pm	Second group 10–11 years bed time.
9.30 pm	Third group 12 years bed time.

A girl that was put to bed at 8.30 pm came and said she has a toothache. I had her brush her teeth and gave her a tylenol, I will send her to the infirmary in the morning.

10.00 pm   Fourth group 13 years and up bedtime.

The scheduled and unscheduled duties and demands addressed by this one child care worker in the course of a single day with twenty-four girls who were well-behaved, according to her diary entry, serves to underline just how hard-pressed child care workers were to keep pace with the daily routine of the residence. There was little time or training that permitted child care workers to offer specialized counselling for individual children with problems. Other cottages were not always as orderly as this particular one was on the day in question. Indeed, during the first three months of the 1985–86 school year, 111 students at the centre were reported to have been absent without permission ("runaways") on 228 different occasions.

The study concluded that PASR (which became PAISEC during the course of the investigation) was the singlemost utilized child care facility available to Indian bands in the Prince Albert district. Taking into account the high proportion of children at PAISEC who had been admitted for social reasons, this institution was actually providing substitute child care for more than one and a half times the number of children in the district whom INAC had otherwise placed in care with provincial social services authorities. Therefore, the first recommendation of the study was that the social development and child care functions of PAISEC be given formal recognition over and above the centre's officially acknowledged educational responsibilities.[11] Another was that staffing levels at PAISEC be raised dramatically in order to approximate the staffing ratios (ranging between five and eight children per child care staff member) common in provincial group homes, receiving homes and residential treatment centres. The doubling of the child care staff at PAISEC would have reduced its staffing ratio to twelve children per child care worker.

Other recommendations in the report called for the enhancement of the quality of treatment offered to children through additional staff training and development; allowing staff representatives to visit each student's family at least once a year in their home communities; expansion of recreational and cultural programs at the centre; and the development of group homes in Indian communities to gradually reduce the need for substitute child care in Prince Albert.

Defining PAISEC's Mission

The administrative process by which PASR was transformed into PAISEC was negotiated over a number of years and at several different levels stretching from the district and regional levels of INAC to the federal treasury board and back to the PADCC. A senior member of the PASR administrative staff, one of a number of personnel who became employees of PAISEC following the transfer, noted in a memo to the PADCC that the negotiation of transfer conditions was complicated by the relative inaccessibility of the treasury board decision-makers.[12] Verbal commitments made to PADCC by Prince Albert district INAC officials were extensively amended, suspended or reversed at higher levels. The PASR official also corroborated the suspicion that, during the previous ten years, there had been a steady erosion in the number of staff members at the residence, a condition that had tilted the institution towards a stance of "crisis response" rather than a preventive approach towards child development and education. Although repeated annual requests for replacement of lost staff positions had been made by PASR, these requests had been denied on the basis that any extra positions required by the institution would be picked up with the devolution of the residence from INAC to the PADCC. Nevertheless, when it came time to transfer control of the institution to the PADCC, these previous reassurances tended to evaporate. The eleven-year-old "temporary" school block made up of portable trailers had come to symbolize for many observers the shallowness of INAC's commitment to helping the people of the PADCC transform PAISEC into an institution that would serve the purposes and meet the goals set for it by Indian governments.

The insistence of federal decision-makers upon alternately denying or at least minimizing the social development functions that had become such a defining feature of PASR's operations meant that PAISEC was labelled and funded as though it was simply an educational institution. A PADCC analyst noted that INAC's draft proposal to establish family and child care services called for funding based upon an average per diem cost of $35.00 per child in settings ranging from foster care to intensive institutional care.[13] If this funding formula had been applied to PAISEC, it would have been possible to immediately double the child care staff at the centre and provide in-service staff training to PAISEC personnel, which would have equipped them to deal more expertly with the social and behavioural difficulties suffered by so many children admitted to the institution. Since this did not happen at the time of transfer, PADCC and PAISEC officials were thereafter placed in the unenviable position of having to seek yearly funding from INAC merely to maintain existing levels of programming and staffing at the centre. Federal officials preferred to keep PAISEC on an exceedingly short financial leash, which might be drawn in abruptly whenever it suited their purposes.

In spite of these persisting financial and structural constraints, PADCC and PAISEC personnel demonstrated a commitment to meeting the objectives set for the centre. During PAISEC's first year of operation much time and effort went into consolidating the complex administration of a centre that now included both educational and child care programs as well as administrative and maintenance functions.[14] In addition to making PAISEC accountable to Indian leadership at both the band and PADCC levels, the centre also completed the year within budget and with a growing reputation in the local business community for paying for supplies and services considerably faster than did government agencies. PAISEC administrators also took pride in acquiring many supplies for the centre at better rates than when these acquisitions had been administered directly by INAC. Under PADCC direction the centre managed to add several staff positions, including two relief child care workers hired with funds previously designated for covering overtime payments to staff members. A ten-week training course (with classes held at the centre one day each week) was organized for child care staff, and an extensive study of the overall child care program (cited above) was completed and subsequently discussed in detail with the child care staff.

The educational component of PAISEC had been expanded through leasing the entire Queen Elizabeth School, a measure that permitted approximately 300 of the normal enrolment of 336 students[15] to attend PAISEC-controlled schools. At Queen Elizabeth a good library had been established along with a fully equipped art and music room. Overcrowded classrooms had been largely eliminated, and an additional gymnasium had been acquired for physical education purposes. The PAISEC schools competed in local school sports leagues in wrestling, volleyball and basketball. An initiative had been launched to facilitate the inclusion of the Indian Culture Program into all subject areas, and a larger review of curriculum was nearing completion. PAISEC's schools were also being employed as the sites for various teacher training programs offered for the benefit of band-controlled schools in the Prince Albert district.

Opportunities for participation in a broader range of after-school recreational activities were expanded beyond the traditional focus on boys' team sports to include crafts, old-time dancing, roller-skating, ringette and weight-lifting. At the same time, PAISEC hockey and soccer teams competing in Prince Albert community sports leagues enjoyed particularly successful seasons with both boys' and girls' teams winning a number of city championships, tournament championships and bronze and silver medals. While PAISEC's first year had not been without its problems, there was ample evidence of a determination to improve programming at the centre and undertake innovations that would improve the quality of care and education provided to Indian boys and girls.

In its second year PAISEC commissioned outside consultants to conduct management and personnel reviews in virtually all of the centre's operations. The review by a chartered accountant of the centre's material acquisition, distribution and control procedures recommended a number of means for tightening and streamlining financial management.[16] A social worker's assessment of child care and kitchen personnel procedures identified several areas of difficulty and provided detailed assessments and recommendations concerning the performance and value to the centre of individual management personnel.[17] The scope of this report—which dealt with issues ranging from the general nature of PAISEC's communications channels and authority structures to specific

Table 6.1
Reasons for Admission of Students to PAISEC, 1988.

Admission Categories	Number of Students	Percentage of Total Student Enrollment
Education*	100	21.4%
Social problems/Discipline	123	26.3%
Single parent	8	1.7%
Unsuitable home atmosphere**	95	20.3%
Migratory family	68	14.6%
Poor housing	11	2.4%
Grandparents raising children***	40	8.6%
Medical reasons****	4	0.9%
Parents in school*****	18	3.9%
Total Students	**467**	**100.00%**

*	"Parents prefer PAISEC as an educational alternative."
**	"Atmosphere not suitable for child's learning (i.e., rest and homework)" or "home environment prevents child from attending school regularly."
***	"Raised by grandparents who do not have the academic skills to support a grandchild's education."
****	"Parents ill and unable to care for the child."
*****	"Parents in school and do not have the financial resources to support child."

Source: PX 113, 1988, PADCC Review of the Operations of the Prince Albert Indian Student Education Centre.

matters concerning the overnight supervision of cottage dormitories, the unstated expectation that staff members would volunteer some off-duty time to facilitate recreational programs, and the question of whether meals ought to be served in the centre's dining hall or in the cottages—served to underline the complexity and challenges inherent in running a residential child care facility.

A review of the management of PAISEC's educational program recommended closer co-ordination between the centre's schools and child care workers, and further noted that the initial set of policy and personnel procedures provided to PAISEC by the PADCC would need to be amended to meet the specific require-ments of an educational facility.[18] PAISEC's school program also suffered a more than $150,000 decrease in funding from INAC during the 1986–87 year as federal officials moved to fund this program on an equal basis with other schools. Yet, since the centre was a residential facility that admitted and discharged students throughout the year in response to social and domestic emergencies in the children's home communities, this meant that a great many more children passed through PAISEC and its schools in a given year than were recognized by INAC's average attendance funding formula. Nevertheless, the schools were obliged to provide books and supplies to each student regardless of the length of their stay at the centre. Moreover, INAC's previous provision of slightly higher rates of funding for ninety-three children who had been classified as being "low cost handicapped" had been withdrawn on the basis that equitable treatment had to be extended to all band-controlled schools. What this action failed to take into account was the unique nature and mission of PAISEC and the increasingly challenging nature of the needs of many of the children who were assigned to the centre.

A review of the centre's student health services carried out in 1986 by two medical doctors and PADCC representatives recommended that the collection of complete medical histories for each student become a standard feature of the admission procedure.[19] Measures for accomplishing this were outlined, and it was noted yet again that the centre's child care staff needed to be increased so that additional attention could be given to individual children. This concern with securing appropriate medical and social development services for PAISEC students intensified throughout the remainder of the 1980s as it became painfully apparent that a significant number of students sent to the centre had previously been abused in their home communities.

To their credit, PAISEC personnel took the lead in addressing these troubling patterns of abuse:

> This abuse takes the form of sexual abuse, incest, physical abuse, mental abuse and various forms of neglect. These issues are sensitive and potentially explosive, since they deal with social fabric and values of the family and larger community. But, we must think about abuse, discuss abuse, and have a course of action that deals with the abuse of children.[20]

The voluntary disclosure to PAISEC staff members of instances of abuse suffered by sixty-nine children subsequently assigned to the centre underlined the extent to which the institution was dealing with issues far beyond the routine provision of educational and residential services. These developments also underlined the urgent need for specialized training that would permit PAISEC teachers and staff to handle disclosures in a socially-sensitive and legally-responsible manner. Accomplishing this would require the investment of time, effort and courage, for there was no instant solution to resolve the many problems mixed up with child abuse. Because PAISEC staff members had been working for some time to determine effective ways of responding to issues of abuse, they comprised one of the PADCC's chief resources for confronting these issues not only in Prince Albert but also at the community level. A PADCC resolution adopted unanimously in November 1987 called for PAISEC staff to make their services available to bands as deemed necessary:

> Whereas there are serious health and social matters which are a result of child abuse cases in the Prince Albert District,
>
> Whereas Prince Albert Indian Student Education Centre has developed a degree of expertise in the area of child abuse,
>
> Whereas the health and social development workers at the Band level have requested the services of P.A.I.S.E.C. staff to deal with child abuse cases,
>
> Be it resolved that on the request of the Prince Albert District Bands, P.A.I.S.E.C. personnel be made available to assist Bands in dealing with abuse cases . . . .[21]

In view of the growing social development responsibilities being shouldered by PAISEC staff, PADCC leaders agreed to a further study of the centre's operations in conjunction with a larger assessment being conducted by INAC and tribal councils of Indian-controlled residential education in Saskatchewan. As Table 6.1 illustrates, the 1988 study of PAISEC demonstrated that the majority of the children at the centre were there for other than strictly educational reasons

The study reported a gradual increase in the proportion of older children enrolled at PAISEC, a trend that necessitated greater expenditures upon food and clothing by the centre. It also reiterated a number of previously identified operational requirements—including the doubling of the child care staff—that needed to be recognized and supported by INAC. Up to this point federal officials had responded to PAISEC's previous requests for temporarily increased staffing with the creation of an on-the-job training program funded by the Work Opportunity Program.[22] This undertaking, which was designed to create a pool of partially-trained Indian child care workers who might subsequently be employed on reserves, did provide some much-needed assistance to PAISEC in the short run, but there was no guarantee that it would be permanently maintained. In the meantime, the supervision of trainees became an additional responsibility for already overburdened PAISEC staff members.

Within the centre's school program a number of significant gains had been registered, including a course of Cree language studies for children in all grades. But while much had been accomplished, much remained to be done, particularly in the field of special education. PAISEC had come to serve a substantial number of special needs and handicapped students who required extra attention in the classroom. The study noted that the school's limited resources for special education were also being tapped to provide extensive English as a second language (ESL) services for children. Finally, the "temporary" facilities provided by the school block at the centre had become plainly inadequate. The major reason provided for not proceeding with the construction of a new school on the reserve land occupied by PAISEC was uncertainty concerning the future role and function of the centre.[23] The reluctance of INAC to make any commitment to the long-term operation of PAISEC was obviously constraining the operations of the centre both as an education centre and as a social development facility.

Educational Functions and Social Development Responsibilities

The focus of the PADCC's study of PAISEC differed significantly from that of a review of Indian student residences in Saskatchewan (including PAISEC), jointly undertaken at the same time by INAC and the Federation of Saskatchewan Indian Nations (FSIN).[24] While recognizing that the Indian Act[25] provided for the operation of Indian student residences, and acknowledging that the use of such institutions for meeting the social and educational needs of Indian children was by no means a recent development, the joint study was inclined to assess the operations of these institutions from the perspective of federal policy and funding guidelines. From this standpoint, the students who attended PAISEC during the 1987–88 school year were identified in the following terms: approximately 70 percent were identified as coming from communities where band, federal or provincial schools could have been utilized by the students who were sent to Prince Albert; approximately 25 percent were classified as being obliged to move to Prince Albert to receive elementary and/or secondary education due to a lack of educational facilities in their home communities; and approximately 5 percent were deemed to be technically ineligible for admission to PAISEC because they were either from out-of-province or from Indian families who resided in off-reserve communities.[26]

The terms by which children were categorized in the joint study recognized only the educational functions served by PAISEC and the other Indian student residences. The underlying message was that students at PAISEC were ordinary children whose ordinary educational needs could be met as well in one educational facility as in another. From this perspective, one might well have concluded that 75 percent of the students at the centre during the 1987–88 school year either came from communities where suitable educational facilities already existed or were technically ineligible to attend a federally-funded Indian student residence. This reasoning implied that the operation of PAISEC was redundant except for approximately a quarter of its current student enrollment. This set of bureaucratic classifications systematically ignored the social development needs that were shared by so many of the children admitted to PAISEC. Although the joint study briefly noted the admissions criteria adopted by the PAISEC Board of Directors, it thereafter overlooked the distinctive needs of the children from the Prince Albert district who would were admitted to the centre on the following priorized basis:

1. Children who are orphans;
2. Parents or guardians who are migratory;
3. No suitable home is available on the reserve;
4. Home is isolated and removed from day school facilities;
5. Socially unstable family situation; and
6. Medical reasons.[27]

Clearly, there were two quite different understandings of the nature of PAISEC and the projected need for its services. According to INAC, PAISEC was merely an old-fashioned Indian student residence that might have been required in the past when many Indian bands in northern Saskatchewan had no access to suitable local educational facilities but which would become entirely obsolete when arrangements for local schooling of on-reserve children in the Prince Albert district were finalized. This view of PAISEC was supported by INAC's custom of funding student residences from its education budget. Since the federal government chose to separate its education and social development programs, it effectively ignored non-educational purposes and functions within these institutions. Just as federal officials had abruptly chosen in 1902 to re-label Emmanuel College as just an "ordinary" boarding school following Rev. Taylor's demand for adequate federal support of that school as a treaty right (as recounted in Chapter 2), so too did their successors exhibit a rigid bureaucratic unwillingness to recognize and accommodate unique needs and situations. Instead of facilitating an innovative First Nations' educational and social initiative, federal officials retreated behind their bureaucratic categories and distinctions in order to manipulate and marginalize an initiative that moved beyond their understanding and imagination.

Yet the staff at PAISEC could not help but be aware of the distinctive mission of their institution and the serious social needs of so many of the Indian children admitted. While band schools had gradually been established in most Indian communities in the Prince Albert district, their capacity to deal with the social and behavioural difficulties experienced by many of the children remained quite limited. In order to meet the needs of these children fully within their home communities each local school would have to employ teachers and child development personnel specially designated for this purpose. However, the cost of adding these capacities to band schools was not allowed for in INAC school funding formulae. Moreover, each community would have to provide suitable forms of residential accommodation and supervision for children who could not be left in their own homes. Thus, the specialized educational, child care, medical, counselling and supervisory services provided to children at PAISEC would have to be duplicated in each band community if the principle of maintaining all Indian children in their home communities was to be rigorously observed.

If these specialized services were not supplied to Indian communities, then local band schools and families would struggle to meet the needs of some of their children and would eventually have to make other arrangements for educating and caring for individual boys and girls. Discussions about introducing band-controlled Indian child and family services programs had been underway for a number of years, but by 1988 not one band in the Prince Albert district had finalized plans to enter into this program field. Therefore, children whose needs could not be satisfied locally would have to be sent out of the community. As long as PAISEC existed, these children could be sent to an Indian-controlled educational and social development facility that was responsible to Indian governments and parents, sensitive to the social and cultural needs of Indian children and experienced in responding to many of the difficulties that afflicted an increasing number of Indian children. In the absence of PAISEC, these children would have to be taken into care under provincial authority and placed in a variety of foster home, group home and intensive care settings, which tended to be staffed primarily by non-Indians.

From the perspective of the PADCC, then, PAISEC was not only an educational facility but, more importantly, a safety net that functioned to keep Indian children from falling into a non-Indian system of child protection that tended to permanently separate a significant proportion of them from their families and communities. While the entry of bands into the provision of Indian child and family services might eventually provide local service for the needs of some of the children sent to PAISEC, it was not certain when this would happen or whether it would, in fact, entirely replace the services provided by PAISEC in the foreseeable future. In the meantime, even INAC's figures established that PAISEC had the lowest average cost per unit of all residential facilities operated for Indian children.[28] In fact, the cost per unit for operating PAISEC during the late 1980s was only about 80 percent of the combined *average* cost incurred by all Indian student residences. As the largest of these institutions then operating in Canada, PAISEC's high enrollment provided it with an impressive economy of scale, notwithstanding the demanding nature of the specialized tasks it performed.

Confronting the Federal Bureaucracy

The release of the joint study sparked a strong reaction among Indian leaders in the province who interpreted it as an undeclared initiative by INAC officials to force closure of the student residences. Accordingly, a meeting was convened in Prince Albert in September 1989 between Assistant Deputy Minister of

Indian Services, John Raynor, INAC and the representatives of the student residences. At this meeting Indian leaders made presentations concerning the specific objectives and characteristics of each institution,[29] along with a submission that identified their shared concerns with the original report of the joint study.[30] The submission began by noting that the so-called "joint" study of Indian student residences in Saskatchewan had been a misnomer, for the report of the findings of this study had not, in fact, been jointly prepared. Raynor was asked at the outset to alter the title of the study to "clearly indicate exclusive INAC authorship."[31]

What followed in the submission was a detailed critique of the assumptions and methodology contained in the original program review:

> The review does not appear to recognize the validity and importance of a holistic education which includes the best possible education, care, skill development and other opportunities that will prepare students to live in both the Indian and non Indian world.[32]

INAC was criticized for arbitrarily separating social development and educational considerations in its assessment of the residences, and the argument presented by federal officials that a shift from educational to social development purposes would require new authorization from Parliament was rejected. The ongoing use of residences for social development functions was not, it was noted, a departure from past departmental practice. Objections were also expressed concerning an informal departmental "freeze" that seemed to have been placed on capital spending for the residences. In view of the serious structural shortcomings of the buildings, this action had placed the future operation of these facilities in doubt. In conclusion, the residences' submission identified and then offered its own answers to three fundamental questions that needed to be raised concerning the future operation of Indian student residences:

1. *Is there a new authority required to provide services to Residences?*
   The finding of this study clearly indicated that no new authority is required.

2. *What are the capital needs for the present and future of Residences?*
   As reported in our commentary, each Residence has a complete assessment of their capital and facility requirements. These assessments must be fully addressed by INAC.

3. *Why has the provision of additional classrooms on Reserves not reduced the demand for admission to residential schools?*
   Clearly the need for Residences is not solely an educational question. As long as bands do not have community infrastructures such

as Child and Family services, proper housing, child intervention programs, acceptable socio economic standards of living, a portion of the student body presently enrolled in the Residences will require the continuation of these services.[33]

Assistant Deputy Minister Raynor assured the meeting that he had learned a great deal about the importance of the student residences to Indians in Saskatchewan and that he would be personally conveying their messages to INAC headquarters in Ottawa.[34] The time had come, noted Raynor, to end the uncertainty about the future of the student residences and to come to an agreement about how to unravel "some of the critical issues that face the Indian education system in Saskatchewan and the place of the student residences in that system." Yet having said this, Raynor committed INAC to little more than maintaining the current rate of funding for student residences "pending a much better understanding of how the education system in Saskatchewan is going to evolve and what role student residences are required to play in the future."

Raynor claimed to have been convinced by the presentations he had heard on the vital roles played by student residences in providing both educational and social services, and observed that it would be wrong to close the residences down "when there are no better solutions in sight." While he acknowledged that INAC did have the authority to fund students placed in residences for social reasons, he viewed this as a "stop-gap" measure:

> the real solution to children that require . . . help and protection is the creation of Indian child welfare agencies. . . .
>
> As you know there are some discussions under way with the provinces to see how Indian-controlled agencies can be developed on Indian reserves. If this could be achieved, it would provide a better solution for the children that are placed in student residences, because there is nowhere else to go. Such Indian agencies would also provide employment opportunities in Indian communities.[35]

On the issue of capital funding, Raynor promised that health and safety issues would be addressed without delay. But the large sums needed to repair and extend the physical structures of the residences would have to be evaluated in terms of Saskatchewan's overall education program allocation. In short, although Raynor appeared to be entirely conciliatory he actually committed INAC merely to continue to fund PAISEC and other student residences for the time being. He did not accept the premise that PAISEC ought to be involved in providing specialized social development services to Indian children except as a "stop-gap" measure. The student residences would be left to grapple with the same problems that they had been struggling to resolve for years.

The Creation of the Counselling Unit

Although questions of policy can be alternately debated or deferred by bureaucrats for years, the difficulties and demands of children cannot be denied by those who work with and care for them on a daily basis. Shortly after Raynor's departure from Prince Albert, officials of the PADCC had to confront operational problems that had surfaced at PAISEC. The unwillingness of INAC to fund more than one student counsellor position at PAISEC left the centre unable to cope with an outbreak of serious behavioural problems among its students in the fall of 1989:

> Crises in student behaviours intensified to the point that an assessment was requested in late October, 1989. Students were acting out, not accepting authority, being disruptive at school, using abusive language, causing property damage, fighting, and many were suspended from school programs. Solvent abuse had been identified as the major contributor to the crises.[36]

A social worker with training in family counselling was contracted to conduct an assessment of child care and educational programs at the centre, identify and organize immediate staff training programs and set up a program for assessing and counselling special needs students.

This initiative provided some immediate relief to the centre and also prompted a number of significant structural changes. To begin with, the management structure of PAISEC was adjusted,[37] and steps were taken to improve communications between child care staff and the school programs operated by PAISEC. An emergency counselling unit was established at the centre with limited term funding provided by INAC. The counselling unit rapidly established a counselling service for individual children as well as a day program to deal with "out-of-control" children. INAC also reluctantly provided temporary support to fund two child care workers for each dormitory of twenty-four children. Finally, in June 1990 approval was given for the implementation of a Satellite Home Program through which sixteen children who were deemed to be at "high risk" were placed in private homes in Prince Albert under the supervision of the counselling unit.[38] These children also continued to receive intensive therapeutic counselling from PAISEC.

From 1990 onward the efforts of PAISEC staff were directed primarily toward improving the standard of services provided by the child care, education, counselling, administrative and maintenance units at the centre. In the fall of 1990 the purchase of Queen Elizabeth School (subsequently renamed, the Angus Mirasty School[39]) by the PADCC and rental of facilities from the Separate School Board in Prince Albert permitted PAISEC both to close the sixteen-year-old "temporary" school block at the residence and provide schooling for all of its children in Indian-controlled classrooms. This marked the first time that

115

Indian children sent to Prince Albert for residential schooling were not obliged to attend non-Indian schools in order to complete elementary and secondary schooling. Admissions to the centre were restricted to children who were members of the twelve bands that made up the Prince Albert district, and a maximum enrollment of 336 students was set for PAISEC. Throughout the 1990s the centre continued to operate within its budgets and developed a knack for discovering ways of making its resources stretch as far as possible. It remained the most cost-effective student residence operating in Saskatchewan, but its administrators were forced to work diligently in order to obtain minimum levels of financial support from INAC.[40]

PAISEC continued to reassess and improve the effectiveness and efficiency of various program areas on a regular basis. In 1992 the counselling unit was the subject of a detailed assessment, which found that it had not evolved significantly since first being set up on an emergency basis in early 1990.[41] Most of the resources of the counselling unit had been applied to providing intensive counselling for individual students and supervising the Satellite Home Program, with little being done in the way of preventive counselling or staff training. Concern regarding the confidentiality of information obtained during consultations with students had apparently led to a lack of communication and co-ordination of efforts between child care workers, teachers and counselling unit personnel. Although demand for individual counselling remained high and the services provided here seemed to be of suitable standard, it was suggested that the counselling unit was stuck in a mode better suited to deal with emergency situations. What was needed now was an emphasis on preventive work with groups of boys and girls that might serve to head off the development of serious difficulties at an earlier stage and, thereby, allow more effective use of counselling resources.[42]

The assessment recommended that many of these problems be resolved by converting the counselling unit from a fee-for-service contractual operation[43] to one where all members of the unit would become PAISEC staff members. This arrangement would permit the establishment of a confidential but co-ordinated means for monitoring the situation of individual children through their interaction with staff in the dormitories, classrooms and counselling programs.[44] The adoption of these recommendations, along with the introduction during the 1993–94 school year of a preventative developmental guidance program to be offered through PAISEC's schools (specifically, Angus Mirasty and the Boucher School facility which was leased from the Separate School Board), signalled an important turning point in the centre's approach to meeting the social needs of its students. The guidance program offered classroom, small group and individual counselling on topics ranging from drug, alcohol and substance abuse to anger management, family life and family violence prevention.[45] The program also initiated routine discussions of issues of social, emotional and spiritual development as well as those involving child and adolescent development and human sexuality.

The Campaign to Close PAISEC

These and other program developments, which clearly identified PAISEC's evolution as a social development and educational facility, were not, however, welcomed by INAC officials. The department's long-term objective of phasing out residential institutions such as PAISEC through the implementation of band or tribal council-controlled Indian child and family service agreements was pursued relentlessly by regional INAC officials from 1993 onwards. Although PAISEC had time and again declared the provision of social development services to Indian children to be an essential and definitive part of its mission, INAC officials resurrected the old argument that there was no mandate for the centre to be involved in these types of activities. Requests made by the Prince Albert Tribal Council (PATC) (which, after 1993, became known as the Prince Albert Grand Council or PAGC)[46] for modest increases to extend the centre's programming (including increased night security at the centre) were rejected by INAC officials without explanation.[47]

Early in 1993 INAC insisted that an independent review team visit PAISEC and review its operations in depth, a request that the centre's management met with full co-operation and free access to staff and records as required.[48] The members of the review team noted the manner in which PAISEC management and staff worked consistently to monitor and improve programming and remarked favourably upon the "tremendous level of concern shown for all children at the residence by all staff interviewed."[49] The review team responded favourably to PAISEC's claims that it required additional funding to accomplish its objectives. Senior regional officials of INAC were distressed that members of the review team might have been misled concerning the legitimacy of PAISEC's operations

> under the premise that we are attempting to fund a child care agency, and have used child care standards to establish recommendations for incremental funding. The reality is that PAISEC has no legal or community mandate to operate such a service and that the majority of children currently in residence are not being screened or sent to the residence for child care services. This conclusion is supported by the fact that 40 students have been returned home by the student residence staff because they "displayed extreme behaviour problems". I would suggest that less than 20% of the current student body could be formally documented . . . [as legitimate] placements with the consent of parents. *Although I cannot prove these "conclusions"* I am concerned that recommendations of this review do not appear to include a concrete action plan to formally (and legally) establish some authority for this facility, other than the recommendation to develope [sic] a joint task team to review the issue. I would further suggest that establishment of PAISEC as an institutional child care facility would not likely be supported by the majority of PATC Chiefs.[50] [emphasis added]

117

Notwithstanding that the review did not substantiate INAC's characterization of the centre, it did provide federal officials with a pretext for registering concern regarding both the staff-student ratios in the centre's schools and the number of children who had withdrawn from PAISEC during the course of the previous school year. In fact, PAISEC had never claimed to be equipped to handle any and all behavioural difficulties. Yet rather than committing their children to the provincial social services system, many bands and parents continued to prefer to send to PAISEC virtually all children who could not be dealt with effectively in their home communities. What was more, given the troubled nature of many of these children, high rates of discharge and withdrawal from this type of facility should scarcely have been surprising. Still, these matters were seized upon by INAC officials and deployed instrumentally as sticking points in their continuing funding negotiations with PAISEC.

In response to the department's professed concern about PAISEC's "unofficial role as a child care facility,"[51] the PATC and PAISEC management devoted considerable time and effort to addressing INAC's demands that the centre establish a protocol agreement with the Saskatchewan Department of Social Services to resolve legal and jurisdictional issues and establish a screening policy that would limit the number of children attending the facility for other than educational reasons.[52] By May 1994 PAISEC had established a rationale for utilization of the centre as a resource for the care of "at risk" Indian children and had adopted internal guidelines and procedures that were entirely acceptable to provincial authorities. Moreover a detailed and sophisticated admission-screening procedure was set in place to ensure that children with dysfunctional behaviours beyond the expertise of PAISEC staff would not be sent to the centre.

Yet in spite of the willingness shown by PAGC leaders and PAISEC managers to respond to whatever objections or concerns INAC officials raised concerning the operations of the centre, it seemed the department was determined to secure the closure of the institution by whatever means possible. In response to an inquiry from a Saskatchewan Member of Parliament concerning the future of student residences, the Minister of Indian Affairs acknowledged that these institutions had previously provided educational as well as child welfare services for Indian children.[53] The minister went on to state that the construction of community-based schools and the provision of additional funds to expand the operation and continue development of Indian Child and Family Service (ICFS) agreements with bands had ended the need for student residences:

> The development of community-based services has, therefore, re-placed the role of the student residences as service delivery agents while the development of local First Nations-controlled schools has diminished the necessity to use residential schools as the only method to provide education for children on reserves.
>
> The history of the Indian student residence has, in many cases, not

been without controversy. You may recall that the government is committed to consult and work with First Nations peoples to identify expenditures that can be redirected to more productive uses for their benefit.[54]

In raising the history of residential schooling in this manner, the minister wittingly or unwittingly employed the bitter memory of past practices by church and state in order to justify the bureaucratically-desired closure of student residences that had only recently been taken over by tribal councils in Saskatchewan. In other words, institutions like PAISEC that had only been in existence for less than a decade were being tarred with the brush of more than a century of state and denominational tutelage. While the minister's declared commitment to consult and work with First Nations' peoples might have been sincerely intended, subsequent developments would demonstrate that his bureaucrats' determination to rid the INAC regional budget of the cost of operating facilities such as PAISEC was not in keeping with the minister's claims.

Given a verbal commitment from the minister that the student residences would not be arbitrarily closed by departmental personnel without full consultation with First Nations authorities, PAGC leaders and PAISEC management opted to undertake yet another review of the institution. This review would include both an assessment of the present and projected future demand for the centre's services by bands in the Prince Albert district and a historical review of the long and complex history of Indian residential schooling in the city.

As the review began, it became apparent that the introduction of Indian child and family services programs in the Prince Albert district was proceeding but would not soon be able to replace the specialized services provided for children at PAISEC. Only a few bands in the PAGC had established their own ICFS programs by 1995, and the experience of those that had commenced suggested that insufficient time was being given to complete staff training and establish a sound foundation for future operations. Instead, INAC and provincial officials seemed to be rapidly and arbitrarily off-loading responsibilities onto the fledgling band social development authorities, despite previous assurances that service transfers would not take place without mutual agreement during the start-up period. The Director of Social Development for one of these bands summarized the situation in this way:

> This is causing pressure on the [band social development] Agency Board and staff to take over services when these services have not been negotiated on. The Agency is in the process of Board Orientation and Staff Orientation to get to know the ropes of the Agency. INAC is not in a position to let the Agency get their feet off the ground. The Provincial Social Services is also in the same position as INAC where the Province wants the Agency to take case transfers.

The Agency is not in a position to take these new services over because we have to get used to the services that we had agreed to take over first before adding other new services to the Agency. The Agency was not consulted nor was the Agency prepared to take on these services that are being dumped on the Agency.

. . . As you can see, . . . the Agency still has quite a way to go until we can get on our feet and be able to stand alone.[55]

Subsequent meetings with regional INAC officials revealed their determination to effect the closure of PAISEC as soon as possible, even though by the department's own criteria this was the one student residence in Saskatchewan that legitimately provided both child welfare services and educational services for boys and girls from band communities that lacked sufficient classroom space and programming.[56] The arbitrary imposition of an unofficial freeze on educational capital expenditures was effected by INAC regional officials on the basis that the capital requirements identified by student residences made it impossible for INAC to meet its previous commitments to band schools. The adoption of this strategy of isolating the student residences and making it appear that their funding requirements were preventing the completion and expansion of band schooling demonstrated that regional INAC officials were prepared to employ a "divide and conquer" strategy in order to impose their own priorities upon Indian communities.

Consideration was not given by federal bureaucrats to what would be in the best interests of Indian children during the development of suitable ICFS programs in the Prince Albert district. Moreover, they did not give any recognition to the commitment and accomplishments registered by Indian people in transforming PAISEC from an institution that had emerged from an unfortunate history of church- and state-operated residential schooling into an Indian-controlled and operated centre that had reversed the unacceptable assumptions and practices of the past. Instead, federal officials imposed their own budgetary priorities and preferred operational categories in a manner that systematically dismissed not only PAISEC's mission as cumulatively determined by Indian leaders and parents, but also the importance of its staff members' continuing efforts on behalf of the children of the Prince Albert district. In August 1995 INAC officials extracted an agreement-in-principle from a meeting with some PAGC representatives to close PAISEC within two years and, in turn, build a band school serving a single community and a limited number of group homes within the district. However, no provision was made to replicate within local communities the specialized and integrated child care, counselling and schooling services provided at PAISEC. Evidently, now, as in the time of Rev. Taylor, an institution that strays beyond the narrow confines of the bureaucratic mindset with respect to federal Indian administration places itself in a highly vulnerable position.

Notes

1. Documentation for this section of the report was obtained primarily from the records of PAISEC. Copies of documents taken from these files have been organized by the author into a provisional classification scheme for reference purposes. Reference to these copied documents will include the designation "PX" and the number of the file into which these copies have been placed.
2. There were, of course, a number of other student residences in Saskatchewan that were transferred to band or tribal council control during the 1980s as well as one that continued to be operated by INAC. Yet each of these institutions had its own specific objectives. PAISEC focused upon the provision of social development services to children more than the other residences did.
3. The federal government was also determined to shift its responsibility for casework with Indian children to provincial authorities. A 1985 draft submission to Cabinet from the Saskatchewan Regional INAC Office calling for decentralization of departmentally administered child care services to permit greater community participation reported that the number of Indian children in Saskatchewan placed in the care of INAC between 1976 and 1985 had fallen from 679 to 334. On the other hand, the number of Indian children placed in care under provincial social services had increased. See PX 140, Submission to Cabinet Child Care Program, INAC, Saskatchewan, Region, prepared by NGA Research Associates, Regina.
4. PX 140, Prince Albert Indian Student Education Centre Child Care Study, Executive Summary, November 1995.
5. Educational reasons included lack of appropriate schooling in the home community or parents following a migratory life on traplines.
6. Social factors for admission included children being orphaned, lack of suitable homes on reserves and unstable and/or impoverished family situations.
7. PX 140, Prince Albert Indian Student Education Centre Child Care Study, Executive Summary, November 1995, p.13.
8. Ibid, p.14.
9. Ibid, p.21–22.
10. Ibid, p.24.
11. Ibid, p.38.
12. PX 117, Student Residence Transfer Program, I. Impey.
13. PX 140, 17 December 1985, P. Brook, PADCC, to H. Bighead and I. Impey, PAISEC.
14. PX 117, 1 May 1986, Prince Albert Indian Student Education Centre Year-End Reports.
15. The official capacity of PAISEC was set at 336 students, reflecting the preferred arrangement of having 24 children in each of the cottage dormitories. In practice, demand for admissions to the school occasionally led to this official capacity being temporarily exceeded.
16. PX 113, 7 November 1986, Prince Albert Indian Student Education Centre, Report on Internal Control Review.
17. PX 113, Duncan Chelsom, M.S.W., A Review of Management/Staff Relations in the Kitchen and Child Care Programs of the Prince Albert Indian Student Residence [sic].
18. PX 113, SERD Consultants, Prince Albert, A Review of the Administrative Structure of the Prince Albert Indian Student Education Centre: Education Program.

19. PX 120, 15 December 1986, PAISEC Health Review, Final Review, July 8, 1986–December 5, 1986.
20. PX 127, 15 June 1987, Abused Students, Prince Albert Indian Student Education Centre.
21. PX 121, 14 November 1987, PADCC Resolution 60–87.
22. Ibid, p.4-5.
23. Ibid, p.11.
24. By 1988 seven of the nine Indian student residences operating in Canada were located in Saskatchewan. See PX 115, 1988, Student Residence Review: A Joint Research Review of Six Indian Student Residences in Saskatchewan. Prepared for and by the Department of Indian and Northern Affairs Canada and the Federation of Saskatchewan Indian Nations.
25. Sections 114(1–2) and 115 of the Indian Act provided for the operation of Indian student residences.
26. Interestingly, the combined percentage figures for all of the six Indian student residences included in the joint study were: 72 percent coming from communities where band, federal or provincial schools could have been utilized by the students who were sent to student residences; 12 percent were classified as being obliged to attend Indian student residences in order to receive elementary and/or secondary education due to a lack of educational facilities in their home communities; and 16 percent were deemed to be technically ineligible for admission to Indian student residences because they were either from out-of-province or from Indian families who resided in off-reserve communities. PX 115, 1988, Student Residence Review: A Joint Research Review of Six Indian Student Residences in Saskatchewan. Prepared for and by the Department of Indian and Northern Affairs Canada and the Federation of Saskatchewan Indian Nations, p.28.
27. Ibid, p.14.
28. Ibid, p.58.
29. The submission made by PAISEC recommended, among other things, that INAC increase its funding of the centre to reflect the actual costs being incurred in operating the facility (see PX 130). A submission made on behalf of the Lac la Ronge Indian Band by Chief Harry Cook noted that some 111 of its children were attending PAISEC during the 1989–90 school year. Although these children were being sent to Prince Albert for a variety of reasons, the band had not developed a formal position on the continued existence of PAISEC. Specifically, Chief Cook noted that the funding of the centre out of the INAC education budget reduced funding to band schools by approximately $5,000–$6,000 for each boy or girl who was assigned to PAISEC: "In other words, it becomes a major dilemma where economics and finance (i.e., financial viability of the Band education program) must be weighted against social and program concerns..." (PX 114, 21 September 1989, Presentation to Assistant Deputy Minister, INAC, by Harry Cook, Chief, Lac La Ronge Indian Band, Saskatchewan respecting INAC Study on Indian Student Residences, p.2.)
30. PX 130, 21 September 1989, Statement to John Raynor, Assistant Deputy Minister of Indian Services, by the Steering Committee of the Participating Student Residence Authorities.
31. Ibid, p.2.
32. Ibid, p.3.

33. Ibid.
34. A typed copy of Raynor's address to the meeting was subsequently faxed to Indian representatives in Saskatchewan. See PX 136, 20 November 1989, H. Billingsley, Indian Services, INAC, Ottawa, to C. Sanderson, FSIN, Prince Albert.
35. Ibid, p.2–3.
36. PX 100, June 1992, Prince Albert Indian Student Education Centre, Counselling Unit Assessment, Final Report, p.8.
37. Earl Ermine was appointed interim director of PAISEC on November 14, 1989, a position he held until July 1990 when he was replaced by Jerry McLeod. Howard Bighead was appointed to serve as co-ordinator of band and community liaison. Louis Ledoux was appointed as principal. See PX 136, 8 November 1989, Chief Ron Michel, Chairman, PADCC Education Board, to Prince Albert District Chiefs, Education Coordinators, and PAISEC Staff, p.1.
38. PX 100, June 1992, Prince Albert Indian Student Education Centre, Counselling Unit Assessment, Final Report, p.11.
39. Angus Mirasty was a Cree elder and former FSIN senator who had long taken an interest in educational issues. He had also frequently visited PAISEC classrooms to discuss Cree culture with the students.
40. See SERD Consultants, Indian Student Residence Resourcing Mechanism Study, September 1991.
41. PX 100, June 1992, Prince Albert Indian Student Education Centre, Counselling Unit Assessment, Final Report, p.11.
42. Ibid, p.60.
43. Ibid, p.68. In fact, up to this point the co-ordinator of the counselling unit and other counsellors had been paid for individual consultations but not for group work, staff training or attending general staff meetings. The fee-for-service arrangement for funding the counselling unit had been hastily adopted during the rush to respond to the behavioural problems shown by so many students at the centre during the 1989 fall term.
44. Prior to 1992 comprehensive records of various staff members' dealings with and observations of individual children were not kept. This made it difficult to approach teaching, child care or counselling in a holistic manner.
45. PX 125, September 1993, Anthony Pynenburg, Developmental Guidance Program for Angus Mirasty/Boucher Schools, 1993–1994 School Year.
46. The Prince Albert District Chiefs Council (PADCC) evolved into the Prince Albert Tribal Council (PATC) in 1992. The following year the PATC was succeeded by the Prince Albert Grand Council (PAGC)
47. PX 125, 1 March 1993, P. Brook, Executive Director, PADCC, Prince Albert, to M. Savill, Regional Director General, INAC, Regina.
48. PX 125, March 1993, PAISEC Review.
49. Ibid, p.2.
50. PX 125, 25 April 1993, A. Bemister, INAC, to M. Savill, Regional Director General, INAC, Regina.
51. PX 125, 17 May 1993, M. Savill, Regional Director General, INAC, Regina, to P. Brook, Executive Director, PADCC, Prince Albert.
52. PX 125, 18 April 1994, R. Gamracy, District Director, INAC, Prince Albert, to P. Brook, Executive Director, PADCC, Prince Albert.
53. PX 124, 12 August 1994, R. Irwin, Minister of Indian Affairs and Northern

Development, to L. Taylor, M.P., House of Commons.

54. Ibid, p.2.
55. PX 124, 13 January 1995, C. Caisse, Director of Social Development, Lac La Ronge Band, to P. Brook, PAISEC Review Team.
56. PX 124, 6 February 1995, P. Brook, PAISEC Review Team, to J. McLeod, Director, PAISEC, p.2.

Chapter 7

Conclusions

This study has intentionally focused upon the operational or administrative dimension of Indian residential schooling in Prince Albert from 1867 to 1995. Its objective has been to provide a comprehensive outline of past and present forms of residential schooling for Indian children in a city that grew up around a Presbyterian mission established for evangelical and educational purposes. Without an understanding of this long and complex history of residential schooling, it is difficult to comprehend how the present-day Prince Albert Indian Student Education Centre came into existence. Moreover, the remarkable achievements registered by Indian people at PAISEC in ten short years to reverse more than a century of assimilationist purposes can be best appreciated when these are systematically contrasted to the previous direction of residential schooling for Indian children by church and state.

As noted in the introduction, this account has intentionally not assumed the task of recording and depicting the personal memories that attendance at various residential schools once operated in Prince Albert or at PAISEC have held for former students. The personal interviews conducted in the course of this study have shown just how much information and insight former students, parents and Indian leaders have to offer concerning these matters. Hopefully the Prince Albert Grand Council will address the need for such an undertaking in the not too distant future. Combining oral accounts with this operational history would provide the basis for producing a remarkably complete historical and cultural record of a field of activity that has been of fundamental importance for so many individuals, families and communities in the Prince Albert Grand Council.

This study has located and reviewed available archival documents and publications that shed light on the history of Indian residential schooling in Prince Albert. Although not all pertinent documents have been made available for examination at this time, the materials examined provide sufficient detail to permit the creation of a reasonably reliable operational history[1] and to identify several important themes and findings that emerge from this historical account.

Indian parents and band leaders have had an abiding interest in obtaining appropriate formal schooling opportunities for their children from the time of the founding of Prince Albert in 1866. Rev. James Nisbet had to seek permission to build his mission and enroll Indian children in his boarding school, and he did so only after concluding detailed discussions with Indian leaders and parents. Aboriginal peoples' interest in educational issues was further demonstrated during the negotiation of Treaty Six when the provision of educational services was insisted upon by Cree spokesmen. Moreover, the establishment of Emmanuel College as a government-funded boarding school for Indian children in the early 1890s was supported by Chiefs from the Prince Albert district.

In later years, Indian parents and leaders continued to monitor the operations of Indian residential schools as best they could even when government policies explicitly sought to use these institutions to separate Indian children from their parents, communities and cultures. Indians were not unaware of the treatment extended to their children in institutions that were controlled by denominational authorities on behalf of the federal government. However, until the 1970s, their concerns were generally ignored by church or state.

The federal government and denominational agencies that played such prominent roles in the management of Indian residential schooling in Prince Albert from the nineteenth century until quite recently have tended to operate on the presumption that they know what is best for Indians. Notwithstanding the good intentions and the responsiveness to Aboriginal concerns by some government and denominational personnel, the structural disempowerment of Indians that has been fundamental to the administration of Indian residential schools created an intolerable situation.

While both church and state professed to be primarily concerned with the welfare of Indians, in fact, both bodies pursued a variety of other institutional objectives through their involvement in Indian residential schooling. Churches, for instance, laid down foundations for subsequent denominational growth by actively evangelizing Indians. Moreover, government financing of church-operated residential schools provided a basis for extending the influence of denominations. The use on two occasions of church-owned facilities for residential schooling in Prince Albert also brought substantial financial benefits to the Diocese of Saskatchewan.

Federal officials who oversaw the development and operation of Indian residential schools exercised control through programs of coercive tutelage. While justifying the department's right to exercise arbitrary power over Indian children, families and communities, these officials steadfastly sought to minimize expenditures. This continuing practice created a situation in which the standard of residential schooling provided to Indian children in Prince Albert was systematically kept beneath acceptable levels. Nevertheless, the economic benefits that have been realized by the city for nearly a century as a consequence of the operation of residential schools for Indians have never been properly recognized or acknowledged by civic officials or business leaders.

This study has also demonstrated that residential schools in Prince Albert were clearly and regularly used by the federal government to provide social services that were not otherwise made available in Indian communities. Although departmental officials have subsequently implied that this was not the case, there is substantial documented evidence of this practice.

The efforts of Indian leaders to take over residential schooling in Prince Albert, especially since the late 1960s, have been undertaken in the general absence of support by federal officials for the principles of either Indian control of Indian education or of Indian parents' right to determine what is best for their children, notwithstanding the bureaucratic rhetoric that might suggest otherwise. Indeed, the survival and development of PAISEC into an accomplished and highly professional educational and social development facility for Indian children has been an accomplishment of the people of the Prince Albert Grand Council. Federal officials have employed a variety of tactics in their attempts to thwart the efforts of the PAGC to build PAISEC into an institution fundamentally unlike the residential schools that preceded it. The evidence indicates that the traditional presumption of federal officials that they know better than Indian parents what is in the best interests of their children has continued to shape the federal government's treatment of PAISEC.

Finally, the accomplishments that have been registered by PAISEC during its short existence deserve to be recognized as positive and encouraging evidence of the capacity of First Nations to design innovative, efficient and holistic institutions to resolve the ongoing social problems that have been engendered by traditional forms of Canadian Indian administration. When viewed in the context of the overall history of Indian residential schooling in Prince Albert, the efforts of the leaders and staff who have worked tirelessly to transform PAISEC to serve the needs and purposes of Indian families and communities represents a remarkable achievement. Their efforts and successes will need to be remembered and emulated in the future.

Notes

1 . There will, no doubt, be information uncovered in the future that may be added to this account. Until that happens the account provided here will offer the most complete outline of the administrative history of residential schooling in Prince Albert currently available.

Bibliography

Abrams, Gary. 1966. *Prince Albert: The First Century, 1866–1966*. Saskatoon: Modern Press.

Ahenakew, Edward. 1973. *Voice of the Plains Cree*. Ed. Ruth M. Buck. Toronto: McClelland and Stewart.

Assembly of First Nations. 1994. *Breaking the Silence: An Interpretive Study of Residential School Impact and Healing as Illustrated by the Stories of First Nations' Individuals*. Ottawa: Assembly of First Nations.

Barman, Jean. 1986. "Separate and Unequal: Indian and White Girls at All Hallows School, 1884–1920." In J. Barman, Y. Hebert and D. McCaskill, eds., *Indian Education in Canada: Volume 1: The Legacy*. Vancouver: University of British Columbia Press.

Bear, Shirley. 1991. "Boarding School Life." In Jack Funk and Gordon Lobe, eds., . . . *And They Told Us Their Stories: A Book of Indian Stories*. Saskatoon: Saskatoon District Tribal Council.

Boon, T.C.B. 1962. *The Anglican Church From the Bay to the Rockies: A History of the Ecclesiastical Province of Rupert's Land and Its Dioceses*. Toronto: Ryerson Press.

Bull, Linda R. 1991. "Indian Residential Schooling: The Native Perspective." *Canadian Journal of Native Education* 18(supplementary):3–63.

Caldwell, George. 1967. *Indian Residential Schools: A Research Study of the Child Care Programs of Nine Residential Schools in Saskatchewan*. Ottawa: Canadian Welfare Council and the Department of Indian Affairs and Northern Development.

Canadian Conference of Catholic Bishops. 1995. *Let Justice Flow Like a Mighty River: Brief by the Canadian Conference of Catholic Bishops to the Royal Commission on Aboriginal Peoples*. Ottawa: Canadian Conference on Catholic Bishops.

Cariboo Tribal Council, Roland Chrisjohn, et al. 1991. "Faith Misplaced: Lasting Effects of Abuse in a First Nations Community." *Canadian Journal of Native Education* 18(2):161–97.

Carter, Sarah. 1990. *Lost Harvests: Prairie Indian Reserve Farmers and Government Policy*. Montreal/Kingston: McGill-Queen's University Press.

Choquette, Robert. 1995. *The Oblate Assault on Canada's Northwest*. Ottawa: University of Ottawa Press.

Dunning, Robert. 1966. *A Century of Presbyterianism in Saskatchewan, 1866–1966*. Prince Albert: St. Paul's Presbyterian Church.

Dyck, Noel. 1986. "An Opportunity Lost: The Initiative of the Reserve Agricultural Programme in the Prairie West." In F. Laurie Barron and James B. Waldram, eds., *1885 and After: Native Society in Transition*. Regina: Canadian Plains Research Centre.

___. 1991. *What is the Indian "Problem": Tutelage and Resistance in Canadian Indian Administration*. St. John's: Institute of Social and Economic Research, Memorial

University of Newfoundland.

Fiske, Jo-Anne. 1991. "Gender and the Paradox of Residential Education in Carrier Society." In Jane Gaskell and Arlene McLaren, eds., *Women and Education: A Canadian Perspective*. Edmonton: Detselig Enterprises.

Friesen, Gerald. 1987. *The Canadian Prairies: A History*. Toronto: University of Toronto Press.

Furniss, Elizabeth. 1995. *Victims of Benevolence: The Dark Legacy of the Williams Lake Residential School*. Vancouver: Arsenal Pulp Press.

Getty, Ian A.L. 1974. "The Failure of the Native Church Policy of the CMS in the North-West." In R. Allen, ed., *Religion and Society in the Prairie West*. Regina: Canadian Plains Research Centre.

Gould, Sydney. 1917. *Inasmuch: Sketches of the Beginnings of the Church of England in Canada in Relation to the Indian and Eskimo Races*. Second edition. Toronto: Missionary Society of the Church of England in Canada.

Grant, John Webster. 1984. *Moon of Wintertime: Missionaries and the Indians of Canada in Encounter since 1534*. Toronto: University of Toronto Press.

Gresko, Jacqueline. 1975. "White 'Rites' and Indian 'Rites': Indian Education and Native Responses in the West." In A.W. Rasporich, ed., *Western Canada Past and Present*. Calgary: McClelland and Stewart.

___. 1986. "Creating Little Dominions Within the Dominion: Early Catholic Indian Schools in Saskatchewan and British Columbia." In J. Barman, Y. Hebert and D. McCaskill, eds., *Indian Education in Canada: Volume One: The Legacy*. Vancouver: University of British Columbia Press.

___. 1992. "Everyday Life at Qu'Appele Industrial School." In Raymond Huel, ed., *Western Oblate Studies 2*. Lewiston/Queenston/Lampeter: Edwin Mellen Press.

Haig-Brown, Celia. 1988. *Resistance and Renewal: Surviving the Indian Residential School*. Vancouver: Tillacum Library.

Hendry, Charles E. 1969. *Beyond Traplines: Towards an Assessment of the Work of the Anglican Church of Canada with Canada's Native Peoples*. Toronto: Anglican Church of Canada.

Hooper, W.J.S., and L.J. Fournier. 1955. *The Development of Educational Institutions in Prince Albert*. Prince Albert: Prince Albert Golden Jubilee Committee and the Prince Albert Co-operative Association.

Jaine, Linda, ed. 1993. *Residential Schools: The Stolen Years*. Saskatoon: University of Saskatchewan, Extension Division.

Lewis, Maurice H. 1966. "The Anglican Church and its Mission Schools Dispute". *Alberta Historical Review* 14(4):7–13.

Logan, Bernice. 1993. *The Teaching Wigwams, Book 2*. Dartmouth: Burnside Publishing.

Marceau-Kozicki, Sylvie. 1993. *Onion Lake Indian Residential Schools, 1892–1943*. Unpublished masters thesis, History Department. Saskatoon: University of Saskatchewan.

Miller, J.R. 1996. *Shingwauk's Vision: A History of Native Residential Schools*. Toronto: University of Toronto Press.

Moore, Rev. William. 1873. *Report on the Condition and Working of the Prince Albert Presbyterian Missions to the Indians on the Saskatchewan*. Ottawa: A.S. Woodburn, Steam Book and Job Printer.

Morris, Alexander. 1880. *The Treaties of Canada With the Indians, Including the Ne-*

gotiations on Which They Were Based, and Other Information Relating Thereto. Toronto: Belfords and Clarke.

Murray, Jean E. 1956. "The Early History of Emmanuel College." *Saskatchewan History* 9(3):81–101.

Newton, William. 1897. *Twenty Years on the Saskatchewan.* London: Elliot Stock.

Nisbet, James. 1869. "Three and a Half Years of an Indian Mission." Saskatoon: Morton Manuscript Collection, University of Saskatoon Archives.

Nock, David A. 1988. *A Victorian Missionary and Canadian Indian Policy.* Waterloo: Waterloo University Press.

Oliver, Edmund H. 1934. "The Presbyterian Church in Saskatchewan, 1866–1881." *Transactions of the Royal Society of Canada* 28 (11):61–94.

Payton, W.F. 1974. *An Historical Sketch of the Diocese of Saskatchewan of the Anglican Church of Canada.* Prince Albert: Anglican Diocese of Saskatchewan.

Persson, Dianne. 1986. "The Changing Experience of Indian Residential Schooling: Blue Quills, 1931–1970." In J. Barman, Y. Hebert and D. McCaskill, eds., *Indian Education in Canada: Volume One: The Legacy.* Vancouver: University of British Columbia Press.

Regnier, Robert, and Peter Legg. 1977. *Our Children Are Waiting: A Study of Federal and Band Operated Reserve Schools in Saskatchewan, Volumes 1 and 2.* Saskatoon: Saskatchewan Indian Cultural College, Education Liaison Department.

Royal Commission on Aboriginal Peoples. 1993. *Special Consultation With the Historic Mission Churches.* Unpublished consultation document for Special Consultation With the Historic Mission Churches. Ottawa, November 8–9.

Sluman, Norma, and Jean Goodwill. 1982. *John Tootoosis: A Biography of a Cree Leader.* Ottawa: Golden Dog Press.

Smith, Derek. 1992. "Governmentality, Indian Residential Schools, and the Canadian Policy of Aggressive Civilization in the Late Nineteenth Century Northwest Territories." Unpublished paper presented at the Canadian Anthropology Society Annual Conference. Montreal, May 9–12.

Smith, Trefor. 1995. "John Freemont Smith and Indian Administration in the Kamloops Agency." *Native Studies Review* 10(2):1–34.

Titley, E. Brian. 1986. *A Narrow Vision: Duncan Campbell Scott and the Administration of Indian Affairs in Canada.* Vancouver: University of British Columbia Press.

___. 1992. "Dunbow Indian Industrial School: An Oblate Experiment in Education." In Raymond Huel, ed., *Western Oblate Studies 2.* Lewiston/Queenston/Lampeter: Edwin Mellen Press.

Tobias, John L. 1983. "Canada's Subjugation of the Plains Cree, 1879–1885." *Canadian Historical Review* 64(4):519–48.

___. 1986. "The Origins of the Treaty Rights Movement in Saskatchewan." In F. Laurie Barron and James B. Waldram, eds., *1885 and After: Native Society in Transition.* Regina: Canadian Plains Research Centre.

Usher, Jean. 1971. "Apostles and Aborigines: The Social Theory of the Church Missionary Society." *Social History* (4):28–52.

Wasylow, Walter Julian. 1972. *History of Battleford Industrial School for Indians.* Unpublished masters thesis, Faculty of Education. Saskatoon: University of Saskatchewan.

Weaver, Sally M. 1981. *Making Canadian Indian Policy: The Hidden Agenda.* Toronto: University of Toronto Press.

Index

1885 Rebellion 13, 15n, 16, 19, 22

Abuse 108-09, 10
  Abusive behaviour by students 45, 100, 115
  Sex-related offences 90
  Sexual abuse 90
  Zimmerman, George Albert 90, 94n

Admission to residential schools 110, 122n, 111, 116, 117
  Criteria 59-61, 121n
  Non-educational purposes and functions of schools 38, 59-61, 72, 75-76, 78, 79, 90, 98-99, 121n, 105, 108-09, 113-14, 115, 117, 120, 125-27
  Placement and admission process 43, 49, 108
  Screening policy 59,91,100
  Troubled children 108
  Unstable and/or impoverished family situations 38, 59-61

Adoption 93

Agriculture
  Agricultural demonstration farm 21
  Emmanuel College [farm and gardening activities] 21-22, 26, 27, 31n
  Federal reserve agricultural [program] 16, 19
  Non-agricultural ways of life 40
  School farms 40, 57
  Vocational training in agriculture 21, 27, 36, 42

Ahenakew, Edward 33n
Ahtahkakoop Reserve 31n
Aklavik (Fort Norman Agency, NWT) 58
All Saints Indian Residential School 41, 51n, 54, 56, 12
Angus Mirasty School 115, 116
Assembly of First Nations 10

Assimilation
  Cultural genocide 86
  De-tribalization 24, 27, 31n
  Forced assimiliation 14, 19 22, 27, 85, 88
  Marriages among graduates of residential schools 25-26
  Moral and cultural engineering 61, 96
  Moral, social and educational development 22
  Separating Indian children from their parents, communities and cultures 14-15, 20-21, 23, 24, 29, 97, 112

Battleford Industrial School 22, 23, 29, 34, 49n

Behaviour and social development
  Behaviour 39-40, 57, 90
  Behaviour and personality problems 45, 73, 90, 98, 100, 105, 115, 123n
  Discipline 23, 100
  Disciplinary problems 43, 47, 55, 56, 79
  Orphans 38, 59-60
  Petty thievery 43
  Punishment 23, 39, 45, 84n
  Solvent abuse 115
  Truancy 38, 43, 47, 75, 104
  Vandalism 38, 39, 55, 90, 115

Bighead, Howard 93n, 93-94n, 123n
Boarding homes 75-76, 83n
Boucher School 116
British North America Act 14
Bramwell, Rev. W.E. 73-75
Bryce, P.H. 28
Caldwell, George 78-80
  Caldwell Report 78-80, 86, 98

Carleton Agency 49n, 51n

Chrétien, Jean 80

Church Missionary Society 22, 31n

Churchill Reserve (Manitoba) 59

Coalition of Saskatchewan Indian Student Residences 91

Community relations [within the City of Prince Albert] 46, 74, 91, 92, 106

    Civic finances 74, 83n

    Contributions to the economy of Prince Albert 41, 91-92

    Economic benefits 74, 91-92, 126

Cook Chief Harry 112n

Cote Reserve 58

Counselling services 116

    Emergency counselling unit 115

    Fee for service 116, 123n

    Preventive counselling 116

    Sattelite Home Program 115, 116

Cree

    Cree language 45

    Cree language instruction 20, 89, 109

    Cree leaders 17, 26, 125

Day schools 18, 23, 27, 29, 40, 61, 72, 96

Dene students 100

Department of Mines and Resources 34, 54

Diefenbaker, John 76, 80

Duck Lake Boarding School 27, 31n, 49n

Elkhorn Residential School 41

Ellis, Rev. H. 36, 38, 50n

Emmanuel College 10, 12, 16ff, 111, 125

Ermine, Earl 123n

Federal funding of Schools

    Allowances too students 72

    Appropriate levels of funding 54

    Capital grants 87

    Financial benefits to the Diocese of Saskatchewan 22, 29-30, 32n, 34-36, 48n, 80, 93n, 126

    Government financing of church-operated residential schools 14

    Increased government funding 76-77

    Levels and quality of staffing 25, 38, 41, 42, 43, 44, 47, 51n, 56, 73, 75,77, 79, 90, 93, 98, 100, 104, 105, 109, 117

    Operating deficits 27, 32n, 58

    Operational costs of residential schooling 44, 58, 61

    Overcrowding 36-38, 39, 40-41, 56, 58, 72, 106, 120

    Per capita grant funding 25, 26, 31n, 27, 28, 55, 57, 58, 71

    Poor classroom facilities and equipment 25, 37, 41, 53n

    Pupilage 23-24, 26, 36, 37, 41-42n, 58-59, 72, 121n

    Reduced government funding to residential schools 25, 26, 28, 29, 32n, 34, 35, 42, 57, 78, 81n, 93, 97, 98, 105, 107-08, 111, 113, 114, 117, 119

    Shortcomings of food and clothing provided to pupils 43, 45, 54, 80n, 81n

    Substandard buildings 25, 27, 28, 38, 44, 47, 54-55, 56, 57-58, 73, 105, 113, 114

    Substandard living conditions 27-28

    Transportation costs 45-46

Federation of Saskatchewan Indian Nations 110

Federation of Saskatchewan Indians 86

Fee-paying high school 21, 30, 34

Fisher, Rev. G.W. 41, 42, 43, 44, 45

Foreign Mission Committee of the Presbyterian Church 17

Foster care 100

Foster homes 112

Goldade, Larry 93n

Gordon's Indian Residential School 39, 46

Gordon's Reserve 58

Group homes 104, 112

    Provincial group home facilities 104

Half-day system 27, 40, 41, 46, 72

Health and safety issues 114

    Bronchitis 28

    Mumps 44, 52n

    Infectious diseases 25, 28

    Measles 28

    Medical and social development services 25, 108

    Mortality rates among pupils 17, 28, 32n

    Pleurisy 28

    Pneumonia 28

    Quarantine 28

    Sanitary conditions 27-28

    Scarlet Feaver 28

Scrofula 28
Student health 37-38
Tuberculosis 25, 28
Hudson's Bay Company
12, 16, 20
Indian Act 110
Abolition of 85ff
Indian controlled agencies
9, 114, 117, 188-20, 127
Band-controlled child
and family services 111-
12,113-14
Band-controlled
schools 10, 120, 122n
Child-care workers 90-
91, 100ff, 106, 107, 108,
109, 115, 116
Holistic education
123n
Indian self-government
9
Indian-controlled
education 71ff, 82n, 88ff,
105-06, 109, 115-16, 120
Special-needs students
110
Study on Indian
Student Residences 113
Indian parents and leaders
9, 10, 13, 59, 82n, 88, 120
Involvement with
schools 9, 23, 29, 30, 43,
56, 71, 76, 78-79, 88, 89,
95-96,100, 104 120, 125-
26, 127
Pupil's contact with
their families 44, 57, 79,
90
Industrial school [for
Indian children] 23
Integrated schooling 71ff,
79, 86-88, 89
Informal educational
ghettoes 86
Treatment of Indian
children 74
James Robert'sReserve
31n

James Smith Reserve 31n,
59
John Smith Reserve 28,
31n, 59
Jones, Miss [matron, St.
Albans] 45
Kamloops Indian Residen-
tial School 82
Key Reserve 59
Lac la Ronge 29, 32n, 34,
37, 39, 40, 51n, 56, 59, 99,
122n
Ledoux, Louis 123n
Little Pine Reserve 59
Little Red River Reserve
40
Lloyd, Archdeacon 29
Mackay, Rev. J.A. 26, 30,
32n
Mackay, Archdeacon John
20, 23, 24, 25, 31n
Martin, H.D. [Bishop of
Saskatchewan] 71
Mayo, Mr. [principal, All
Saints] 45
McLean, Bishop 18, 20,
21-22, 29
McLeod, Jerry 123n
Métis 12, 13, 20
Military base
Basic Training Camp
40, 41ff, 54, 56, 73, Ex-
122
Minister of Citizenship
and Immigration 54
Mirasty, Angus 89, 123n
Missionary Society of the
Church of England in
Canada 36, 38, 40, 41, 43,
44, 45, 47, 48, 49n, 51n,
54, 57,58, 72, 73
Mistawasis, Chief 22
Mistawasis Reserve 31n,
58
Moore, Rev. William 17-
18, 30n
Moosomin Reserve 59
Mosquito-Grizzly Bear

Head Reserve 58
National Indian Brother-
hood 88, 93n
Native Church Policy 20
Native clergy 20, 21
Nisbet, James 17, 18, 30n,
95, 125-26
Ochapowace Reserve 59
Onion Lake 40, 48
Onion Lake Church of
England Indian Residen-
tial School 29, 34, 36, 38,
49n
Opawakoscikan Reserve
92
Ostrander, J.P.B. 37-38
Paternalism 14, 85
Paul, Archdeacon 34-35
Peepeekisis Reserve 58
Peter Ballantyne 59, 92,
99
Pilcher, Rev. N.D. 45, 46-
47
Presbyterian   Mission
Church 12, 16ff
Prince Albert Tribal Council
92, 117, 123n
Prince Albert District Chiefs
88-89, 92
Prince Albert Indian Student
Education Centre 9, 10, 12,
95ff, 121n, 127
Prince Albert Grand Council
7, 9, 10, 11, 12, 15n, 17, 117,
120, 123n, 125, 127
Prince Albert Indian Resi-
dential School 10, 11, 12,
15n, 54ff, 72, 73ff, 86
Reconstruction
project 76-77
Prince Albert Student Resi-
dence 12, 86ff, 93n, 95, 96,
98, 105
Queen Elizabeth School
[see also Angus Mirasty
School] 92, 94n, 106, 115
Queen Victoria 7
Racism

Authoritarianism and racism 13, 19, 30, 44, 54, 96, 126
  Discrimination 91, 92
  Prejudice 35, 41, 50-51n, 71
  The arts of civilised life 17, 23
RCMP 50N, 77
Recreation 99, 100, 107
  Sports 72
  Air Cadets 72, 83n
  Hockey 46, 106
  Indian Culture Program 106
  Recreational facilities 38, 55-56, 106
  Soccer 106
Red Earth Reserve 59
Red Earth Indian Day School 47, 60
Red Pheasant Reserve 58
Roberts, Jim 93-94n
Royal Commission on Aboriginal Peoples 10,
Saddle Lake 49n
Sanderson, Sol 93n
Sandy Lake Reserve 58
Saskatchewan, University of 21, 29
Scrase, Rev. A.J. 45-46
Shoal Lake Reserve 58
Sioux language 30
Smith, Chief James 22, 95
Smith, Chief John 22
St. Alban's Indian Residential School 36ff, 54, 56
St. Alban's Ladies College 30, 34
St. George's Boys Residence 34
St. Mary's Church 20, 21
Stanley Mission 40
Star, Cliff 93n
Starblanket, Chief 22
Sturgeon Lake Reserve 59
Sweet Grass Reserve 59

Taylor, Rev. James 26f, 30, 31n, 111, 120
The Pas Reserve 58
The Pas Indian Day School 60
Theological college 20, 27, 29, 30
Tootoosis, John 43, 52n
Training, vocational
  Forestry work 51n
  New forms of livelihood 19
Treaties 7, 12-13
  Federal government's reneging on treaty commitments 19, 27, 28-29, 111
  Treaty Lands Entitlement program 92
  Treaty obligation 13, 41, 111
  Treaty Six 13, 18, 20, 26, 31n, 45, 125,
  Treaty-making 18ff
  Tutelage 24, 15, 15n, 19, 85, 88, 97, 119, 126, 127
Unpaid Indian labour
  Pupils' labour, farm or domestic chores 24, 40, 42, 46-47, 50n, 51n, 57, 73, 103
Wahpeton Band 89
White Bear Reserve 58,
White Cap's Reserve 59
White Paper 85ff, 93n
Wickenden, Rev. 39
William Charles Reserve, Montreal Lake 31n, 59
William Twatt Reserve 31n

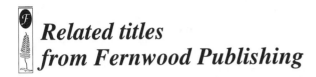

Related titles from Fernwood Publishing

The Míkmaw Concordat
James (Sekej) Youngblood Henderson

This important work, written primarily as a Native Studies text, fills a large gap in the history of Native peoples in the Americas. It is a fascinating multidisciplinary journey covering intellectual history, law, political science, religious studies, and Míkmaw legends, oral history and perceptions from the arrival in America by Columbus and other Europeans in the fifteenth century to the Míkmaw Concordat in the early seventeenth century. There is virtually nothing else in print concerning the relationship between the Míkmaw Nation (or any other First Nation) and the Church during the Holy Roman Empire.

Contents: Discovery and European Thought • Papal Bull Inter Caetera, 1493 • The Black Legend and Civil Laws • Aboriginal Dominion • The Beautiful Trail • National Consolidation • Reflections
120pp Paper ISBN 1 895686 80 6 $14.95

Thunder in My Soul
A Mohawk Woman Speaks
Patricia Monture-Angus

This book contains the reflections of one Mohawk woman and her struggles to find a good place to be in Canadian society. The essays, written in enjoyable and accessible language, document the struggles against oppression that Aboriginal people face, as well as the success and change that have come to Aboriginal communities. It is written from a woman's place. A possible text in a variety of disciplines—women's studies, Native studies, sociology, education, politics and law—it is an excellent book for anyone who wishes to better understand Aboriginal experience. It speaks to both the mind and the heart.

"Monture writes about aboriginal peoples' experiences with education, racism and the criminal justice system, without missing the cultural dilemmas, the role of women in education and the law, or the human factors that make all these experiences more complex." S. Stiegelbauer, *Resources for Feminist Research*
273pp Paper ISBM 1 895686 46 6 $19.95

Names, Numbers, and Northern Policy:
Inuit, Project Surname, and the Politics of Identity
Valerie Alia
When power is unequal and people are colonized at one level or another, naming is manipulated from the outside. In the Canadian North, the most
blatant example of this manipulation is the long history of interference by visitors with the ways Inuit named themselves and their land. This book is a concise history of government-sponsored interference with Inuit identity.
118pp Paper ISBN 1 895686 31 8 $12.95

Elusive Justice: Beyond the Marshall Inquiry
Joy Mannette ed.
"The Marshall Commission Report. . .does not deserve accolades. While it acknowledges errors, negligence and mismanagement, it did not make the connections necessary to begin the process of developing a dialogue about a justice system that Aboriginal people can respect, or which respects Aboriginal people." —M. E. Turpel, Dalhousie Law School
108pp Paper ISBN 1 895686 02 4 $12.95

New from the Latin America Bureau (Available from Fernwood Books):

Return of the Indian: Conquest and Revival in the Americas
by Phillip Wearne

"After 500 years of injustice, 500 years of night, we are moving into the light of a new era for our peoples. We believe that our voices will make themselves heard, that you will listen to us." From the foreword by Rigoberta Menchú, 1992 Nobel Peace Prize Winner

"A great book, educational and informative. It's a must reading for those who are interested in indigenous peoples' issues." Matthew Coon Come, Grand Chief of the Cree, Quebec

"*Return of the Indian* brings together for the first time the present condition of the forty million indigenous people of North, Central and South America. It is a long-needed work that shows the cultural diversity of the two continents as well as significant parallel historical courses." Dee Brown, author of *Bury My Heart at Wounded Knee*
240pp Paper large format   colour / B&W photographs
ISBN 0 304 33458 8 $39.95